SE
THE GREAT EJECTION

SERMONS OF THE GREAT EJECTION

Wherefore I take you to record this day, that I am pure from the blood of all men. For I have not shunned to declare unto you all the counsel of God.
Acts 20:26, 27

THE BANNER OF TRUTH TRUST

THE BANNER OF TRUTH TRUST
3 Murrayfield Road, Edinburgh EH12 6EL, UK
P.O. Box 621, Carlisle, PA 17013, USA

*

An Exact Collection of Farewel Sermons Preached by the late London Ministers (the *London Collection)*
first published 1662
England's Remembrancer first published 1663

This selection first published to mark the
tercentenary of the Great Ejection, August 1962

New revised and reset edition 2012
Reprinted 2012

ISBN: 978 1 84871 152 5

*

Typeset in 10.5/13.5 pt Sabon Oldstyle Figures
at the Banner of Truth Trust, Edinburgh

Printed in the USA by
Versa Press, Inc.
East Peoria, IL

CONTENTS

INTRODUCTION TO TERCENTENARY EDITION, 1962

When the preparation of an Introduction for this book was commenced, it was soon found that the amount of material which needs to be stated regarding the Great Ejection of 1662 is such that it cannot be adequately covered within the limits of a few opening pages. Of the 2,000 ejected from the national Church on St Bartholomew's Day, 1662, some were born in the reign of Queen Elizabeth and others lived to see the times of George I, and just as their lives encompass that wide sweep of history from the last of the Tudors to the first of the Hanoverians—from the sixteenth to the eighteenth centuries—so any serious consideration of the cause and consequences of the Ejection must carry us far beyond the confines of a single year. The Act of Uniformity,[1] which silenced the vast majority of England's

[1] The principal terms required by the Act were: a declaration of 'unfeigned assent and consent' to everything contained in the *Book of Common Prayer*, re-ordination for those not episcopally

evangelical preachers, was no sudden act of kingly folly or parliamentary misgovernment; rather it was the turning point in a great and long-drawn-out struggle. It is necessary to grasp this fact in order to appreciate why that 24th day of August was referred to by our evangelical forefathers as 'Black Bartholomew's Day.' The Ejection was no isolated event of merely temporary significance; it was a spiritual watershed, which divides two eras in our religious history. Such was the conviction of the ejected ministers themselves: 'This fatal Day that deserves to be wrote in Black Letters in England's Calendar,' declared Matthew Mead, and Thomas Lye affirmed what all his Puritan brethren felt in calling the Ejection 'the greatest turn there ever was in England.' These words were not the language of injured self-importance. It was for Christ and not for themselves that these men acted when they gave up all, and they believed that in thus standing out against the conformity that the authorities demanded they were only doing as their Lord required of them. We should greatly underestimate the seriousness of 1662 if we imagined that the cleavage which then took place was only over phrases in the *Book of Common Prayer* and forms of Church order. These things were involved, but the Puritans regarded them as only a part of a much wider issue, namely, what is the nature of true Christianity? The Nonconformists believed that in acting as they did

---

ordained, and a renunciation of the Solemn League and Covenant. Knowing that the Puritans would not submit to such terms, the authorities framed the Act to secure their expulsion.

they were acting for the gospel, and when they were sentenced to be deprived and silenced they felt as John Bradford felt a century before when he wrote, 'The condemnation is not a condemnation of Bradford simply, but rather a condemnation of Christ and his truth. Bradford is nothing else but an instrument, in whom Christ and his doctrine are condemned.' It was for this reason that they took such a serious view of the Ejection; they saw that a turning point had come and that there was cause to tremble for the land's spiritual future.

Our knowledge of what subsequently took place confirms the correctness of their view. Whatever we may think were the weaknesses of the Puritans, there can be no denying that it was their activity that had led to a period in which theology was valued, when sound doctrine and fervent gospel preaching were esteemed, and when Bible reading and spiritual hunger were characteristic of large portions of the common people. It is equally true that after the silencing of the 2,000 we enter an age of rationalism, of coldness in the pulpit and indifference in the pew, an age in which scepticism and worldliness went far to reducing national religion to a mere parody of New Testament Christianity. Such assertions are not just the reflection of a Nonconformist viewpoint, for they have also been frequently confirmed by evangelical Anglican writers. Speaking of the effects of 1662, J. B. Marsden wrote:

> If it be presumptuous to fix upon particular occurrences as proofs of God's displeasure, yet none will deny that a long, unbroken course of disasters

> indicates but too surely, whether to a nation or a church, that His favour is withdrawn. Within five years of the ejection of the two thousand Nonconformists, London was twice laid waste, first by pestilence and then by fire . . . But other calamities ensued, more lasting and far more terrible. Religion in the Church of England was almost extinguished and in many of her parishes the lamp of God went out.[1]

Says Archdeacon Hare,

> After we had cast out so much faith, and zeal, and holiness, after we had in this manner almost cast out the doctrine of Christ crucified from the pale of our church; we had to travel through a century of coldness and dreariness, and barrenness, of Arminianism and Pelagianism, of Arianism and latent Socinianism, all which were found compatible with outward conformity.[2]

In language of similar strength a former Bishop of Liverpool, J. C. Ryle, referred to the Ejection as 'an injury to the cause of true religion in England which will probably never be repaired . . . a more impolitic deed never disfigured the annals of a Protestant Church.'[3]

In view of the extensive historical, spiritual and theological implications which are thus bound up with 1662,

[1] J. B. Marsden, *The History of the Later Puritans* (London: Hamilton, Adams & Co., 1852), pp. 469-70.

[2] *Miscellaneous Pamphlets,* by Archdeacon Hare, p. 37. Quoted by Robert Vaughan, *English Nonconformity* (London: Jackson, Walford & Hodder, 1862), p. 458.

[3] J. C. Ryle, *Light from Old Times* (London: Chas. J. Thynne, 1903), p. 316.

it was decided to reprint the following sermons without any lengthy Introduction and to refer readers to a separate companion book, which is being prepared along those lines.[1] This decision was in harmony with the purpose of this book, which is to let the ejected ministers speak for themselves rather than to attempt to pass our own verdict upon their action. Perhaps no body of men in English church history has in fact been so often sentenced by a prejudiced posterity before they were ever allowed to speak for themselves. They have seldom been accorded the liberty which King Agrippa gave the apostle when he said, 'Thou art permitted to speak for thyself.' There is a sense in which this was literally true three hundred years ago. Some of the Puritans, for example, were never allowed to preach the last words they had prepared to speak in public. The Devon Puritan leader George Hughes, who intended to preach his Farewell at St Andrews, Plymouth, on Wednesday, August 20, 1662, found that the mayor had had the church doors locked against him. Similarly Thomas Jollie of Altham, Lancashire, going to his church to speak his last words as minister of the parish seven days before the legal enforcement of the Act of Uniformity, was forced out of his chapel and a squadron of horse-soldiers settled in the village to see he did not speak elsewhere. The spiritual history of the

[1] The book referred to—*The Death of Two Thousand*, by Iain H. Murray—was never published, but a special 'tercentenary commemoration issue of 1662' of *The Banner of Truth* magazine was produced in June 1962, in which the background to and lessons from the Great Ejection were covered by the same writer.—P.

next quarter century following the Great Ejection is little more than one long record of the attempts of men to silence the scattered Puritan ministers. The Conventicle Acts, the Five Mile Act, the enmity of the Cavalier Parliament, the plots of a popish court, the craftiness of Archbishop Sheldon, the energies of bishops, and the tyrannizing of drunken Judge Jeffries were all towards this end. 'If we keep steady our proceedings,' wrote Lord Herbert in 1682 to urge on the justices in the work of persecution, 'in a short time I believe a Dissenter will scarce be heard of.' By almost every method which men knew, an attempt was thus made to shut the mouths of Nonconformists, and for continuing to claim the liberty to speak not a few of the Nonconformists lost their lives. When at the trial of Vavasor Powell—who had already spent seven years in prison—an appeal was made that he should be released on bail, the crown counsellor immediately raised the crushing objection, 'No, my Lord, then he will go and preach,' and so Powell died in prison. When Thomas De Laune ventured to defend Nonconformity in writing in 1683 he was speedily arrested. At his trial he asked leave to defend his position against any who would confute it —'if what I have written be true, it is no crime, unless truth be made a crime.' But the only answer De Laune got was a criminal's death in stenching[1] Newgate along with his wife and two children.

What a quarter century of fines, prisons and persecutions had failed to do was afterwards attempted by other means. Jest, caricature, sarcasm, and downright

[1] That is, 'stinking.'—P.

lies were all pressed into service to pillory the memory of the ejected ministers. Addison in *The Spectator* depicted the Puritan leader Thomas Goodwin examining students for admission at Magdalen College in a room of gloomy darkness 'with half-a-dozen nightcaps upon his head and religious horror in his countenance.' White Kennett professed to be writing history when he described the majority of the ejected as men of 'morose, clownish, and sullen and reserved natures.' The acid writings of men like Anthony Wood and John Walker were in similar vein—'Mechanicks, and Fellows bred to the meanest occupations' was the latter's estimate of not a few of the Bartholomeans of 1662. Obloquy of this character thrived amidst the moral decline of eighteenth century England, and indeed when Whitefield began his ministry in the late 1730's there was no more effective way of overthrowing his labours, so his enemies thought, than simply to brand him as a would-be restorer of Puritan fanaticism and enthusiasm. Thus even in the eighteenth century Puritanism was rarely given leave to speak for itself.

It is not suprising that this should still be true today even at the tercentenary of their ejection. In so far as the men of 1662 approximated, we believe, more closely to the teaching of the New Testament than any other group of English Christians, it is inevitable that unregenerate men in the professing church and in the world should have no time to hear them. Our Lord's principle is always true, 'For everyone that doeth evil hateth the light, neither cometh to the light, lest his deeds should be reproved' (*John* 3:20). There could be few more scathing reproofs for modern English Christianity than for us really to attend to the words of these men who gave up livings, homes, liberties, goods and sometimes lives rather than surrender any part of the teaching of the Word of God. Their highest ambition was to be able to say with William Tyndale,

> I call God to record against the day we shall appear before our Lord Jesus, to give a reckoning of our doings, that I never altered one syllable of God's Word against my conscience, nor would this day, if all that is in the earth, whether it be pleasure, honour, or riches, might be given me.

Yet although in this tercentenary year various things have been written to commemorate the Ejection, the present writer has yet to see the sentiments of the Bartholomeans stated in their native simplicity and strength. There is no better place to find these sentiments than in the Farewell Sermons which these men preached to their congregations, but far from being quoted these sermons have not even been mentioned, though they are of supreme importance in determining the real feelings of the men who went out. This present reprint, then, is intended to put the reader in *direct* contact with the Ejected. The Puritans were fond of a saying of Bernard's, 'Hast thou appealed unto the Gospel? unto the Gospel shalt thou go,' and in a similar way these pages may say to the many who for differing reasons are celebrating 1662, 'Hast thou appealed unto 1662? Unto 1662 shalt thou go!'

A few words of explanation are required concerning the manner in which the following sermons have been selected. They are taken from the two volumes that were secretly printed by unnamed publishers shortly after the Ejection, the first entitled *A Collection of Farewell Sermons Preached by the late London Ministers* and the second, *England's Remembrancer*, being *A Collection of Farewell Sermons Preached by divers Non-conformists in the Country*. Both works were published in defiance of the control of the press, and despite the activities of the irate Censor of the Press, Roger L'Estrange, the *London Collection* went rapidly through about twelve editions, a fact which gives some indication of the popularity of the men who were silenced. The complete *London Collection* contains between thirty and forty sermons (the editions differ slightly) and the sermons of the country ministers eighteen. Apart from a few other Farewell Sermons which were printed separately, these are all that survive of the many hundreds that were preached in August 1662. Despite the popularity of the *London Collection* it laboured under the disadvantage of being only hearers' notes uncorrected by the preachers; if it had not been for this, the ministers whose names were given could have been soon charged with promoting an illegal publication. In the case of the *Country Sermons,* which are obviously more full, complete and frequently in a better style, it is evident that the ministers themselves had a hand in the publication, and this is confirmed by the complete absence of any means of identifying the preachers. It was only many years after that Edmund Calamy (1671-1732), the Nonconformist historian, was able to name them.

There are many more of the Farewell Sermons deserving of re-publication than are contained in the following pages, and it may be hoped that some day a much fuller edition will be reprinted. Readers may notice the absence of some of the well-known Puritan names in this selection. One reason is that some of the leaders, particularly Independents like Owen and Goodwin, were not in parish churches, and consequently, while they were silenced by the subsequent persecution, they were not put out of congregations by the Act of Uniformity. Another reason is that the last sermons of some of the foremost preachers like William Jenkyn and Richard Baxter, while they were printed, have noticeably suffered at the hands of poor note-takers.[1] It is absurd for a modern writer to say of the Farewell Sermons that 'they all seem to have been forgeries,'[2] for some of them can be proved to be exceptionally accurate reports of what was actually said,[3] but there can

[1] Cf. Richard Baxter, *Reliquiae Baxterianae*, Part II, (London: T. Parkhurst, J. Robinson, J. Lawrence, and J. Dunton, 1696), p. 303.

[2] C. E. Whiting, *Studies in English Puritanism from the Restoration to the Revolution, 1660–1688* (London: Society for Promoting Christian Knowledge; New York: Macmillan Company), 1931, p. 555.

[3] A comparison can be made between a paragraph of William Bates' Farewell Sermon which Samuel Pepys heard and recorded in his *Diary* and the same paragraph as given in the *London Collection*.

be no doubt that in some cases the scribes were responsible for a roughness which gives some of the sermons a slipshod appearance. This has therefore been an additional factor in determining the selection which has been made. The first seven sermons are from the *London Collection* and the last two from *England's Remembrancer*. They have not been abridged, but printing errors, difficult punctuation and occasional obsolete words have been corrected or modernized to improve the readability.

John Stoughton has described the Sunday upon which most of the Farewell Sermons were preached:

> No Sunday in England ever resembled exactly that which fell on the 17th of August, 1662. In after years, Puritan fathers and mothers related to their children the story of assembled crowds, of aisles, standing-places and stairs, filled to suffocation, of people clinging to open windows like swarms of bees, of overflowing throngs in church-yards and streets, of deep silence or stifled sobs, as the flock gazed on the shepherd—'sorrowing most of all that they should see his face no more.'[1]

It is well for us to bear such a background in mind as we read the following pages. The atmosphere of that day was electric and charged with emotion; the popular discontent was great, and strong guards stood ready in London, but these sermons seem far removed from all that. There is a

[1] John Stoughton, *History of Religion in England from the Opening of the Long Parliament to the End of the Eighteenth Century*, vol. III (New York: A. C. Armstrong & Son, 1882), p. 267.

calmness, an unction and a lack of invective. Great though their sorrow was for their flocks and for their nation, they had a message to preach that was more than equal to the strain of the crisis. An eternal God, an ever-living Saviour and a glorious hope of heaven, carried them through this heaviest trial, and the note of joy and triumph with which George Swinnock concluded his Farewell to his people at Great Kimble, Buckinghamshire, leads us to the heart of true Puritanism:

> Now ye have a storm, but hereafter an everlasting calm; now ye are tossed to and fro, and weather-beaten; but faith, by the prospective glass of the gospel, discovers land, and this without question may support your spirits . . . He will never leave you that are his, nor forsake you. I know not to commend you to one so loving; he lived in love, he in our natures died for love. His love is like himself, boundless and bottomless. It is impossible to commend you to one so able; he can supply all your needs, fill all your souls to the brim . . . He can build you up, and give you an inheritance, where all the heirs are kings and queens, and shall sit on thrones, and live and reign with Christ for ever and ever. There ye shall have robes of purity on your backs, palms of victory in your hands, crowns of glory on your heads, and songs of triumph in your mouths; there ye may meet together to worship him without fear and drink freely of his sweetest, dearest favour; there your services will be without the smallest sin and your souls without the least sorrow. If pastor and people meet there, they shall never part more. It is some

> sweet comfort now that though distant in places, we can meet together at the throne of grace; but oh, what a comfort will it be to meet together in that palace of glory! But since we must part here, 'finally, my brethren, farewell; be perfect, be of good comfort, be of one mind; live in peace, and the God of love and peace shall be with you.'[1]

May this book be used to revive preaching like this in England at the present time.

IAIN H. MURRAY
June 27, 1962

[1] *The Works of George Swinnock*, Vol. 4 (Edinburgh: Banner of Truth Trust reprint of the 1868 James Nichol edition, 1992), pp. 99–100.

EDMUND CALAMY

LIFE

Edmund Calamy, born in 1600, was the son of a London citizen. Entering Pembroke Hall, Cambridge, in 1616, he studied assiduously—reputedly sixteen hours a day—and became a Fellow of Pembroke. Despite his scholastic attachments, Calamy's vigorous opposition to Arminianism hindered his path to preferment. He became lecturer at Bury St Edmunds in 1627, where his colleague was Jeremiah Burroughes, but after ten years' faithful ministry, despite his peace-loving disposition, was driven from Bury by Bishop Wren's articles enforcing uniformity and ceremonies. The period of Calamy's great popularity began when, in 1639, he was chosen at St Mary's, Aldermanbury, and here he attracted large congregations, including the wealthy and influential. As one of the authors of the 'Smectymnuus' tract, he wrote against the fashionable doctrine of the divine right of episcopacy and was a member of the Westminster Assembly of Divines. At this time Calamy was established as a Presbyterian leader, and he commonly presided at the meetings of the city ministers.

But although he favoured reform in the church,

Calamy opposed the execution of the king, a position typical of the Presbyterians generally. Accordingly, after Cromwell's death he was one of those who took the initiative in recalling Charles II, and at the Restoration seemed to be in favour at Court, being offered the bishopric of Lichfield and Coventry, which, however, he refused. He still expected a settlement comprehending the Puritans and was one of the commissioners at the Savoy Conference, but his hopes were dashed, and he was duly ejected, as was his eldest son. Calamy continued to attend the services at Aldermanbury and, on the 28th of December 1662, when the preacher failed to appear, was persuaded to fill his place. Though three months after the Ejection, the sermon he preached that Sunday was usually printed with the *London Collection* of Farewell Sermons, and it is reprinted in the following pages. It is a better example of Calamy's preaching than his Farewell sermon, which was imperfectly taken down. It is also some indication of the man's stature that, having come to worship, he could preach in such a manner without prior warning.

As a result of this sermon, Calamy was arrested for disobeying the Act of Uniformity, but released by command of the king because of the disturbance caused by his imprisonment. In 1666 Calamy drove round London and was broken-hearted at the havoc wrought by the Great Fire. He never recovered, and died in the same year.

PRAYER

[*Edmund Calamy's Prayer at Aldermanbury*]

Oh most Holy, thou ever blessed Lord God, thou fillest heaven and earth with thy presence. We pray thee fill all our hearts with the presence of thy grace, and let it appear that thou art in the midst of us, with that powerful assistance of thy Spirit, that we may receive a token of love from thee at this time. It is a singular favour that the doors of thy sanctuary are open to us and that we may meet together in thy name. We pray thee continue it to us, and sanctify it to us, that every sabbath may add to our stature in Jesus Christ.

We confess we have forfeited all our mercies; we have heard much of God, Christ and heaven with our ears, but there is little of God, Christ and heaven in our hearts. We confess, many of us by hearing sermons, are grown sermon-proof; we know how to scoff and mock at sermons, but we know not how to live sermons.

It is a miracle of free grace thou hast not taken thy gospel from us ere this time, but thou art a merciful God, and though we cannot please thee, yet mercy pleases thee; and we have no argument to bring along with us to beg thy favour but thy mercy in Jesus Christ. We pray thee that thou wilt glorify thy sovereignty, in being gracious to us, and pardon our many and great transgressions.

Thou makest use of the malice of men for thy glory; thou killest Goliath with his own sword. Oh, help us to put our trust in thee, thou that canst kill, and cure by killing.

Bless these nations of England, Scotland and Ireland, and find out yet a way to save us. Pour down thy blessing upon the head and heart of our sovereign, Charles, by thy grace, King of Great Britain. Thou hast done great things for him; let him do great things for thee. Bless him in his royal consort, in his royal relations, in his council; bless the magistrates and ministers of this realm.

Lord, forgive us, for we live as if we had been delivered to work wickedness. We cannot sin at so cheap a rate as others do. We pray thee humble us under our great and grievous sins. Give us repentance unto salvation and a lively faith through the blood of Jesus Christ. Quicken our graces, forgive our sins, make alive our souls. Let us be such as thou wilt have us to be. Make us Christians not only by outward profession, but an inward heart-experience, that we may live in heaven while we are on earth and come to heaven when we shall leave the earth.

To that purpose bless thy Word unto us at this time, and give us all grace to make conscience of what we hear and how we hear; and all for Jesus Christ's sake, to whom with thy blessed self and Spirit be all glory and honour, Amen.

TREMBLING FOR THE ARK OF GOD

And when he came, lo, Eli sat upon a seat by the wayside watching: for his heart trembled for the ark of God.
1 Samuel 4:13

That you may the better understand these words, you must know that whatsoever God threatened against old Eli in the second and third chapters, because he did not restrain his wicked sons from their lewd courses, is here executed in this chapter. Therefore we read there were four thousand Israelites slain by the Philistines. The elders of Israel met together to consult how to repair this great loss; they confess it was the Lord that had smitten them. For, they say, 'Wherefore hath the Lord smitten us today before the Philistines?' And they conclude the way to repair this their loss was to fetch the ark of the covenant of the Lord from Shiloh and carry it into the battle. Whereupon they appointed Hophni and Phinehas to fetch it, for they imagined that the presence of the ark would save them from ruin.

But herein they were miserably mistaken. For this judgment came, not because the ark was not in the camp, but because their sin was in the camp. The ark of the covenant would not preserve those that had broken covenant with God. And therefore there was a great slaughter of the Israelites; thirty thousand men were slain, Hophni and Phinehas were also slain, and the ark itself was taken prisoner. But what was old Eli doing? He was ninety and eight years old and was not able to go to the battle, but sits upon a seat by the wayside near the battle; and there he sits, thinking what shall become of the ark. 'And lo, Eli sat upon a seat by the wayside, watching; for his heart trembled for the ark of God,' for fear lest the ark should be taken. He was not troubled what should become of his two sons, or what should become of the people of Israel, but what should become of the ark of God.

In the words of the text are three parts:

1. Old Eli's concern for the ark,

2. Old Eli's trembling for fear of the ark,

3. Old Eli's preferring the safety of the ark before the safety of his two sons, wife and children.

'He sat upon a seat by the wayside watching; for his heart trembled for the ark of God.' But what was the ark of God? Why should old Eli's heart tremble for fear of the ark?

I answer, this ark was the holiest of all the things of God; it was so holy that it made every place holy where it came.

> And Solomon brought up the daughter of Pharaoh out of the city of David unto the house that he had built for her: for he said, My wife shall not dwell in the house of David king of Israel, because the places

> are holy whereunto the ark of the LORD hath come (2 *Chron.* 8:11).

This ark was the dwelling-place of God, it was the habitation of God. 'The LORD reigneth . . . he sitteth between the cherubims' (*Psa.* 99:1). Now these cherubims were placed over the ark; it was the speaking place of God, he met his people there, and there he gave an answer to them.

> And thou shalt put the mercy seat above upon the ark; and in the ark thou shalt put the testimony that I shall give thee. And there I will meet with thee, and I will commune with thee from above the mercy seat, from between the two cherubims which are upon the ark of the testimony, of all things which I will give thee in commandment unto the children of Israel (*Exod.* 25:21, 22).

This ark was God's footstool, and all the people of God worship him before the footstool of God. 'Exalt ye the LORD our God, and worship at his footstool, for he is holy' (*Psa.* 99:5). The ark was also the glory and the strength of Israel. And he 'delivered his strength into captivity, and his glory into the enemy's hand' (*Psa.* 78:61). It was the terror of the enemies of God, and therefore when the ark came into the battle, the Philistines were afraid and said, 'Woe unto us, for God is come into the camp.' And indeed this ark was called Jehovah.

> And it came to pass, when the ark set forward, that Moses said, Rise up, LORD, and let thine enemies be scattered . . . and when it rested, he said, Return,

O LORD, unto the many thousands of Israel (*Num.* 10:35, 36).

In a word, the ark was a pledge and visible sign of God's gracious presence with his people. As long as the ark was safe, they were safe; and when the ark was with them, then God's presence was with them. But when the ark was gone, God was gone—his comforting presence, his protecting presence, and his preserving presence.

It is therefore no wonder that this good old man sat watching here for fear of the ark. I call him good old man, although many are of the opinion that he was not good because he suffered his sons to be wicked; and indeed his fault was great. But surely he was a good man, and I have two reasons to prove it. First, in that he took the punishment of his iniquity so patiently: 'It is the LORD: let him do what seemeth him good.' And secondly, he was a good man, as his care for the ark shows: 'He sat trembling for the ark.'

Now the ark was a type of three things:

First, it was a type of Jesus Christ; for as God spake from the ark, so God speaks to us by Christ.

Secondly, it was a type of the church of Christ; for as the ark was the preserver of the two tables of the law, so the church of Christ is the preserver of the Scriptures.

Thirdly, the ark was a type of the ordinances of Christ; for as God did communicate himself by the ark, so God by his ordinances communicates his counsels, comforts, and grace unto his people. Thus I have showed you what the ark was.

I shall gather two observations from the words of the text:

I. When the ark of God is in danger of being lost, the people of God have thoughtful heads and trembling hearts.

II. A true child of God is more troubled and more anxious what shall become of the ark than what shall become of wife and children or estate.

I shall begin with the first doctrine, namely, that when the ark of God is in danger of being lost, the people of God have thoughtful heads and trembling hearts. Or, if I may put this doctrine in a gospel dress, take it thus: when the gospel is in danger of being lost, when gospel-ordinances and gospel-ministers are in danger of being lost, then the people of God have trembling heads and concerned and anxious hearts about it.

Mark what I say. I say not when the ark is lost; for that was death to old Eli, that broke his neck, and it cost the life of Eli's daughter-in-law. When the ark of God was taken, she took no comfort in her child; though a man child, she regarded it not. For 'the glory is departed from Israel, the ark of God is taken.'

I say not when the ark of God is lost; but I say when it is in danger of being lost. When the gospel is in danger, the ministers of the gospel in danger, and the ordinances in danger of being lost, then the people of God have thoughtful heads and anxious hearts. When God threatened the Israelites that he would not go with them, they were troubled for the loss of God's presence and would not put on their ornaments. 'I will not go up in the midst of thee, for thou art a stiffnecked people: lest I consume thee in the way. And when the people heard these evil tidings, they mourned, and no man did put on him his ornaments' (*Exod.* 33:3, 4). 'And it came to pass, while the ark abode in Kirjath-jearim, that the time was long; for it was twenty years: and all the house of Israel lamented after the LORD' (*1 Sam.* 7:2), that is, after the presence of God, speaking from the ark. In 2 Samuel 11: 10, 11 David would have had Uriah to go down to his house and make merry; but

> Uriah said unto David, The ark, and Israel, and Judah abide in tents; and my lord Joab, and the servants of my lord, are encamped in the open fields: shall I then go into mine house to eat and to drink, and to lie with my wife? as thou livest, and as thy soul liveth, I will not do this thing.

In 1 Kings 19:10 Elijah says,

> I have been very jealous for the LORD God of hosts: for the children of Israel have forsaken thy covenant, thrown down thine altars, and slain thy prophets with the sword, and I, even I only, am left; and they seek my life, to take it away.

Thus you see when the ark is in danger, the people of God mourn and are sorrowful.

There are four reasons why the people of God are so much troubled when the ark of God is in danger.

1. *Because of the great love they bear to the ark of God.* As 'the LORD loveth the gates of Zion more than all the dwellings of Jacob' (*Psa.* 87:2), so the people of God

love the ordinances of God, and the faithful ministers of Christ. 'LORD, I have loved the habitation of thy house, and the place where thine honour dwelleth' (*Psa.* 26:8). 'One thing have I desired of the LORD, that will I seek after; that I may dwell in the house of the LORD all the days of my life, to behold the beauty of the LORD, and to enquire in his temple' (*Psa.* 27:4). Now love stirs up the affections, as young Croesus who, though he were dumb, yet seeing his father likely to be killed, cried out, 'Do not kill my father.' Such is the love of the saints of God to the ark, that they cannot be silent. They cannot but tremble when they see the ark in danger. For Zion's sake, they cannot hold their peace. They cannot be silent until the Lord make 'the righteousness thereof go forth as brightness, and the salvation thereof as a lamp that burneth' (*Isa.* 62:1).

2. The people of God are troubled when the ark is in danger *because of the personal interest they have in the ark of God.* Now interest stirs up affection, just as when a man is concerned when a friend's house is on fire. You had a lamentable and sad providence this last week, and it is not to be forgotten—how suddenly in all our feastings, God may dash all our mirth. Now consider how affected they were that had an interest in those that were burned: so the people of God have an interest in the ark. God is the haven of the children of God, the portion and inheritance of the children of God; and when God begins to forsake them, they cannot but be afflicted and troubled. The ordinances of God are the jewels of a Christian and the treasure of a Christian, and the loss of

them cannot but trouble him. And Jesus Christ is the joy of a Christian, and therefore when Christ is departing, he cannot but be much afflicted by it.

3. The people of God are much troubled when the ark is in danger *because of the mischiefs that come upon a nation when the ark of God is lost.* Woe be to that nation when the ark is gone! The heathen Greeks had the image of Apollo, and they conceived that as long as that image was preserved among them they could never be worsted but must be preserved. The Romans had a buckler, concerning which they had a tradition that as long as that buckler was preserved, Rome could not be taken. I will give a hint of what happens when the ark of God is lost.

When the ark of God is taken, 'the ways of Zion do mourn, because none come to the solemn feasts' (*Lam.* 1:4). This was the complaint of the church and matter of sadness.

When the ark of God is taken, the ministers of Christ are driven into corners. This is matter of heart-trembling.

When the ark of God is taken, the souls of many are in danger.

When the gospel is gone, your souls are in hazard. There is cause of sadness.

When the ark of God is taken, the enemies of God blaspheme and are ready to say, 'Where is your God?' Then do the enemies of God triumph. 'As with a sword in my bones, mine enemies reproach me; while they say daily unto me, Where is thy God?' (*Psa.* 42:10).

When the ark of God is taken, Jesus Christ is trampled under foot, and the ordinances of God defiled and trampled on; and then blasphemy and atheism come in like an armed man.

4. The people of God must needs tremble when the ark is in danger *because they share the responsibility for the losing of the ark*. It was this which made old Eli so much troubled, because he knew it was for his sin that God suffered the ark to be taken. He knew that his own guilt in not punishing his two sons was one cause of that great slaughter the people of Israel met with, and that made him tremble. There is no person here in this congregation, but his heart will tell him that he has contributed something towards the loss of the ark. None of us is so holy but our consciences must accuse us. We have done something that might cause God to take the ark from us, and therefore Mr Bradford, that blessed martyr, said in his prayer, 'Lord, it was my unthankfulness for the gospel, that brought in popery in Queen Mary's days; and my unfruitfulness under the gospel that was the cause of the untimely death of King Edward the Sixth.' Again, those that fled in Queen Mary's days sadly complained that they were the cause of God's taking away the gospel from England. Oh, beloved, it is for your sin and my sin that the ark of God is in danger; and therefore the Lord gives us trembling and burdened hearts as to what shall become of the ark.

I come now to the application.

Use 1. If it is the mark of a true child of God to be concerned when the ark of God is in danger and to have such a trembling heart for fear of the ark, then this is a certain sign there are but few that are the children of God in truth. Oh where is the man and where is the woman that like old Eli sits watching and trembling for fear of the ark? And the reasons for watching and trembling are these:

First, *the many sins in this nation*. For let me tell you, there is not one sin for which God ever took away the ark from any people but it is to be found in England. Did the church of Ephesus lose the candlestick because they had lost their first love? And have not we lost our first love to the gospel and to the ordinances? And did the church of Laodicea lose the candlestick because of lukewarmness? And are not we lukewarm? Did the people of Israel, as here in the text, lose the ark because they abhorred the offerings of God? And do not you do so? Are not the sins of Israel amongst us? And the sins of Germany and the sins of all other nations about us? And is there any man here before God this day, in this congregation, who can consider the great unthankfulness of this nation and the great profaneness and wickedness of this nation and not conclude that the ark is in danger and that God may justly take the ark from us?

I might tell you of the drunkenness, adultery, covetousness, injustice, uncharitableness, and such like sins, that abound among us. I might tell you of sanctuary sins, profanation of sabbath and sacraments, our unthankfulness, and unfruitfulness, and unworthy walking under the gospel. And you of this place, God may very well take the ark even from you; and indeed it was out of the great interest I had in you (which while I live I shall ever own), and from that great affection and respect I had to you, that I would not send you home this day without a sermon and let you go without a blessing. Now can any of you in this parish, and this congregation, can any of you say, God may not justly take the gospel from you?

The second reason for trembling is *the discontents and divisions of the nation.* As Christ says, 'A nation divided against itself cannot stand'; but I leave these things to your consideration. I believe there is none here but will confess the ark of God is in danger of being lost. But now where are our Elis to sit watching and trembling for fear of the ark? Where is the wife of Phinehas who would not be comforted, because the ark of God was taken? Where are our Moseses, our Elijahs, our Uriahs? Where are they that lay to heart the dangers of the ark? You complain of taxes, decay of trading, of this civil burden, and that civil burden, but where is the man or the woman that complains of this misery, the loss of the ark? Most of you are like Gallio; 'he cared for none of these things'; if it had been a civil matter, then he would have meddled with it; but for religion, he cared not for that. Every man is troubled about mine and thine and about civil matters; but who lays to heart, and who regards what shall become of religion? There is a strange kind of indifference and lukewarmness upon most people's spirits. So long as their trading goes on, and their civil burdens are removed, they care not what becomes of the ark.

There is a text of Scripture—I shall not spend much time in opening it, but I would have you well consider it—Hosea 7:9: 'Strangers have devoured his strength, and he knoweth it not: yea, gray hairs are here and there upon him, yet he knoweth not.' Shall I say grey hairs are upon the gospel? I come not hither to prophesy; I say not, the gospel is dying, but I say it has grey hairs; for you have had the gospel a hundred years and above, and therefore it is in its old age. And I dare challenge any scholar to show me an example of any nation that has enjoyed the gospel for a hundred years together. Now, that grey hairs belong to a hundred years is no wonder. Well, grey hairs are here and there, and yet no man lays it to heart.

Now I shall show you what a great sin it is not to be affected with the danger that the ark of God is in. Consider but three particulars:

First, it is a sign you do not love the gospel. If you had any love to it, you would be troubled more for the danger of the ark, than for any outward danger whatsoever.

Secondly, it is a sign you have no interest in the gospel, for interest will stir up your affections. It is a sign you are not concerned in the gospel, for if you were concerned in it, you would be affected with it, as even it was with those that were interested in those persons that were in that lamentable fire last week; it was impossible that they should be unaffected. And so it is a sign you have no interest in God and Christ, if your hearts do not tremble for fear the ark be lost.

Thirdly, there is a curse of God pronounced against all those that do not lay to heart the affliction of Joseph.

> Woe be to them that are at ease in Zion, and trust in the mountain of Samaria . . . ye that put far away the evil day . . . that lie upon beds of ivory, and stretch themselves upon their couches: that eat the lambs out of the flock, and the calves out of the midst of the stall: that chant to the sound of the viol, and invent to themselves instruments of music . . . that drink wine in bowls, and anoint themselves with the chief ointments: but they are not grieved for the affliction of Joseph' (*Amos* 6:1-6).

Woe be to you that enjoy your fulness of outward things, and make merry therewith, and never consider the afflictions of God's people and the danger of the ark.

Use 2. Let me, by way of exhortation, beseech you all whom God by a providence has so unexpectedly brought together this day to hear me (and there may be a good providence in it). I say, let me beseech you all to declare you are the people of God in deed and in truth, by following the example of old Eli, to be very concerned for the ark of God, and let me exhort you to five particulars:

First, let me persuade you to believe that the gospel is not entailed upon England; England has no letters patent of the gospel; the gospel is removable. God took away the ark and forsook Shiloh, and he not only took away the ark, but the temple also. He unchurched the Jews, he unchurched the seven churches of Asia, and we know not how soon he may unchurch us. I know no warrant we have to think that we shall have the gospel another hundred years. God knows how to remove his candlestick but not to destroy it. God often removes the church but does not destroy it. God removed his church out of the East; the Greek churches were famous churches, but God removed them, and now the Turk overspreads that country.

Secondly, I would persuade you that England's ark is in danger of being lost, even were it only for the sins of England, those prodigious iniquities amongst us and that strange unheard-of ingratitude that is in the land. But I will say no more of that, because I would speak nothing but what becomes a sober minister of the gospel.

Thirdly, I would persuade you, and, oh, that I could raise you up to old Eli's practice: 'He sat watching; for his heart trembled for the ark.' He had a thoughtful head and an aching heart for the ark of God that was in great danger. That I might move you to this, consider what a sad condition we are in, if the ark is taken. What good will your estate do you? or what good will your business do you if the gospel be gone? Wherein does England excel other places? There is more wealth in Turkey than in England, and the heathen nations have more of the glory of the world than any Christian king has. What is the glory of England? Is it not Christianity? What is the glory of Christianity but the gospel? If the gospel be gone, our glory is gone. Pray remember Eli's daughter-in-law, the wife of Phinehas. She hearkened not, though a man child was born, and would receive no comfort, but called his name Ichabod, for 'the glory is departed from Israel; the ark of God is taken.' Oh, when the glory is gone, who would desire to live? I am loth to tell you the story of Chrysostom; he was but one man, yet when he was banished from Constantinople the people all petitioned for him and said that they could as well lose the sun out of the firmament as lose Chrysostom from among them.

Fourthly, let me persuade you not to mourn immoderately, neither be discouraged. I would willingly speak something to comfort you before I leave you. I know not by what strange providence I came here this day, and the Lord knows when I shall speak to you again: therefore I would not send you home comfortless. Oh, therefore mourn not as without hope, for I have four arguments to persuade me that the ark of God will not be lost, though it is in danger.

(i). Because God hath done great things already for this nation. I argue like Manoah's wife, Surely, if God had intended to destroy us, he would not have done what he has done for us. He who has done so much for us will not now forsake us. And therefore though our hearts tremble, yet let them not sink within us.

(ii). I argue from the abundance of praying people that are in this nation. There are many that night and day pray unto God that the ark may not be taken; and let me assure you, God will never forsake a praying and reforming people. When God intends to destroy a nation and take away the ark, he takes away the spirit of prayer; but where God gives the spirit of prayer, there God will continue the ark. You all know that if there had been but ten good men in those five cities God would have spared them. We have many hundreds that fear God in this nation, that do not give God rest, but night and day pray unto God for this land. And who knows but for their sakes God will spare the ark?

(iii). Another ground of comfort is that God has hitherto dealt with England, not by way of rule, but by way of prerogative. We have had sins fitted to unchurch us all the reign of Queen Elizabeth and King James, and the godly ministers have been threatened with ruin from year to year; but God has hitherto saved England by way of prerogative. God has spared us because he will spare us, according to that text, 'I will be gracious to whom I will be gracious.' God will not be tied to his own rule, and who knows but God will deliver us again?

(iv). Another ground of comfort is that God is now pouring out his vials upon antichrist, and all this shall end in the ruin of antichrist. God is pouring forth his vials upon the throne of the beast, and all these transactions shall end in the ruin of antichrist. Though some drops of these vials may light upon the Reformed churches, and they may smart for a while, and God may severely punish them, yet it will be but for a little while. God may scourge all the Reformed churches before these vials are fully poured out, and persecution may go through them all; the which I call drops of these vials, but the vials are intended for antichrist. And whatever becomes of us, yet our children and our children's children shall see the outcome of the vials poured out upon the whore of Babylon. This I speak for your comfort.

Fifthly, I am to exhort you that you would all of you contribute your utmost endeavour to keep the ark of God from being taken. And here I shall show you what magistrates, ministers and the people should do.

I shall say but little about what magistrates should do, because I am not now to speak to them. They are to use their authority for the settling of the ark; for the ark of the covenant will be like the ark of Noah, always floating upon the waters, until the magistrates settle it. Thus it was with David (2 *Sam.* 6:1, 2), who gathered together all the chosen men of Israel, thirty thousand, to fetch home the ark. So, too, with Solomon (*1 Kings* 8:1), who assembled the elders of Israel, and the heads of the tribes, the nobles, and the chief of the fathers of the children of Israel at Jerusalem with a great deal of pomp to bring up the ark of the covenant of the Lord into its place. Oh, that God would encourage our nobles and magistrates that they might be concerned to settle the ark. Magistrates must not be as the Philistines; they had the ark, but what did they do with it? They set it up in the house of Dagon, but Dagon and the ark could never agree. Where false religion comes in at one door, true religion goes out at the other. You must not put the ark and Dagon together.

What must the ministers do to keep the ark from being lost?

They must endeavour after holiness. The ark will never stand steady, nor prosper upon the shoulders of Hophni and Phinehas. A wicked, profane, drunken ministry will never settle the ark. It must be the sober, pious, godly ministers that must do it. How holy must they be that draw nigh to the God of holiness!

What must the people of God do, that the ark may not be lost?

There are five things I shall commend unto you, and then commend you to God.

(i) You must not idolize the ark. That was the sin of the people in the text. They thought the very presence of the ark would excuse them and keep them safe, and, therefore, they carried the ark into the camp. Though they reformed not and repented not, yet they thought the ark would save them. So there are many that think the ark will save them, though never so wicked. But nothing will secure a nation but repentance and reformation.

(ii) Do not undervalue the ark. This was Michal's sin (2 *Sam.* 6:14–23). When David danced before the ark, Michal mocked him, and despised him in her heart, 'but,' said he, 'it was before the LORD, and if this be vile, I will yet be more vile.' Some men begin to say, what need have we of preaching? will not reading prayers serve? Others say, what need have we of so much preaching? will not once a day serve? Now this is to undervalue the ark. Therefore let us say as David: If to preach the Word and to fast and pray for the nation is vile, then I will yet be more vile.

(iii) We must not pry into the ark. This was the sin of the men of Bethshemesh. 'They looked into the ark, and God smote them, and cut off fifty thousand and threescore and ten men' (*1 Sam.* 6:19). Be not too curious in searching where God has not discovered or revealed. For example, there are great thoughts of heart as to when God will deliver his people and set his churches at liberty; and many men talk much of the year 1666. Some say that shall be the year in which antichrist shall be destroyed. And there are strange impressions upon the hearts of many learned men as to that year. Some go to the year 1669, and others pitch upon other times. But, truly, if you will have my judgment, and I am glad of this opportunity to tell you, this is to pry too much into the ark. Remember the text, 'It is not for you to know the times or the seasons which the Father hath put in his own power' (*Acts* 1:7). And thus to fasten upon any particular time, if you find you are deceived, this is the way to make you atheists, and thus afterwards you will believe nothing. Those ministers do no service, or rather ill service, to the church of God that fix upon the times and seasons.

A popish author says that in the year 1000 there was a general belief over the Christian world that the day of judgment should be that year; but when they saw it did not happen, they fell to their old sinning again and were worse than before and believed nothing. Well, God's time is the best; therefore let us not pry too much into the ark.

(iv) You must not meddle with the ark, unless you have a lawful call to meddle with it. This was the sin of Uzzah (2 *Sam.* 6: 6, 7). The ark was in danger of falling, and he, good man, meaning no hurt, to support the ark took hold of it; but for so doing, he destroyed himself and made a breach and hindered the carrying home of the ark at that time.

We have had a great deal of disorder heretofore; and an abundance of well-minded people have usurped the ministerial office. They were afraid the ark was falling, and therefore they touched the ark, they laid hold on the ark; but their touching the ark has undone the ark and themselves too. Oh, take heed of touching the ark.

(v) If ever you would preserve the ark, then keep the covenant of the ark; keep the law that the ark preserves. The ark was a place in which the two tables of the law were kept. Keep the law, and God will keep the ark. But if you break the law, you will forfeit the ark. The ark was called the ark of the covenant. Keep covenant with God, and God will preserve the ark. But if you break the covenant of the ark—the covenant made in baptism, and that covenant often renewed in the sacrament—if you break covenant, God will take away the ark.

THOMAS BROOKS

LIFE

A prolific and popular writer, yet one of whose own life little is known, Thomas Brooks was born in 1608. For the details of his home circumstances we are dependent on inferences. The fact that he was able to enter Cambridge in 1625 as a pensioner indicates that his family was in comfortable circumstances; that he was sent to Emmanuel College suggests that they were of Puritan sympathies. It is most probable that while at Cambridge, he attended the preaching of Richard Sibbes and Dr John Preston, then Master of Emmanuel. Brooks himself began to preach regularly about 1640. He seems to have been at sea with the Fleet, and also with the Army, and was Chaplain to Colonel Thomas Rainsborough of the parliamentary army, whose funeral sermon he preached in November 1648. The following month Brooks was called to preach before Parliament. In 1648 he preached at St Thomas Apostle's Church in London, but by 1652-3 was settled as preacher at St Margaret's, Fish Street Hill, where he remained until the Act of Uniformity. At St Margaret's he refused to administer baptism and the Lord's supper indiscriminately, and this provoked an attempt to remove him, which was, however, unsuccessful.

After the Ejection Brooks was pastor of a congregation at the Pavement, Moorfields. When many conforming ministers left London during the Great Plague of 1665, he was active preaching. His old church in Fish Street Hill was the first to be burned down in the Fire which destroyed eighty-seven London churches in the following year, and the event occasioned one of his most moving works, *London's Lamentations*. A few years after his second marriage, Brooks died in 1680. His practical writings, which are of outstanding quality, went into many editions during his own lifetime. *The Complete Works of Thomas Brooks* were reprinted in six volumes with a brief memoir by A. B. Grosart, by James Nichol, Edinburgh, 1866-7. This edition was reprinted by the Banner of Truth Trust in 1980.

A PASTOR'S LEGACIES

All that I shall do shall be to answer two or three questions, and then I shall leave a few legacies with you that may speak when I am not at liberty to speak to you.

Question I. The first question is this, What should be the reason that men make such opposition against the gospel, against the plain, powerful, conscientious preaching of it? This is not the principal thing that I intend, and therefore I shall only touch upon the reason of it. Men's hatred and opposition arises against the gospel:

1. Because it discovers their hidden works of darkness. They hate the light, 'lest their deeds should be reproved' (*John* 3:20). The gospel brings their deeds of darkness to light, and this stirs up a spirit of hatred and opposition against the gospel.

2. Because sinners under the gospel cannot sin at so cheap a rate as otherwise they might do—the drunkard cannot be drunk at so cheap a rate; nor can the opposer and persecutor oppose and persecute at so cheap a rate as they might do where the gospel does not shine in power and glory.

3. Because the gospel puts persons upon very hard service, upon very difficult work, pulling out a right eye, cutting off a right hand, offering up an Isaac, throwing overboard a Jonah, parting with bosom lusts and darling sins. Herod heard John Baptist gladly, till he came to touch his Herodias, and then off goes his head. As they say, 'This is a hard saying; who can hear it?' (*John* 6:60), and from that time they walked no more with him. This is a hard gospel indeed, and at this their blood rises.

4. Because of the differing and distinguishing work that the gospel makes among the sons of men—it softens one, and hardens another that sits next to him; enlightens one and strikes the other blind; it wins one and enrages the other. The same sun has different effects on the objects on which it shines. The gospel puts a difference between the precious and the vile; and this the vile cannot bear. It was never good days, say they, since such and such must be saints, and none else; we have as good hearts as any, and this enrages them.

5. Lastly, it is from Satan. Satan knows that the very tendency of the gospel is to shake his kingdom about his ears. Satan and antichrist know that their kingdom must go down by the power and light of the gospel; and therefore Satan and men of an anti-christian spirit do all they can to oppose and show their hatred against the everlasting gospel; and this makes them to be in such a rage against the gospel.

Question II. When the gospel goes from a people, what goes?

I shall but touch on this matter.

1. When the gospel goes, peace, plenty, and trading go.

Consider 2 Chronicles 15:3-6, 'Now for a long season Israel hath been without the true God, and without a teaching priest.' Why? They had priests; but they were Jeroboam's priests, as you may see,

> Have ye not cast out the priests of the LORD, the sons of Aaron, and the Levites, and have made you priests after the manner of the nations of other lands? so that whosoever cometh to consecrate himself with a young bullock and seven rams, the same may be a priest of them that are no gods (2 *Chron.* 13:9).

A little business will buy a priesthood; and so they are said to be without the true God, without a teaching priest, and without law. Mark what follows in verses 5 and 6:

> And in those times there was no peace to him that went out, nor to him that came in, but great vexations were upon all the inhabitants of the country. And nation was destroyed of nation, and city of city: for God did vex them with all adversity.

2. Safety and security goes when the gospel goes; so in the text last cited. The ark was taken away, and when that was taken away, their strength and safety was gone. When the Jews rejected the gospel, the Romans came and took away both their place and nation: 'If we let him thus alone . . . the Romans shall come and take away both our place and nation' (*John* 11:48). About forty years after, Titus and Vespasian took away their

city. And this was the ready way to bring the Romans upon them.

3. When the gospel goes, civil liberty goes. When the Jews slighted the gospel and turned their backs upon it, they quickly became bondslaves to the Romans.

4. When the gospel goes, the honour and glory, splendour and beauty of a nation goes. It is the gospel that is the honour and glory of a nation, and when that goes, all the glory goes. As old Eli said,[1] when the ark was taken away, 'The glory is departed from Israel' (*1 Sam.* 4:21). 'Hath a nation changed their gods, which are yet no gods? but my people have changed their glory for that which doth not profit' (*Jer.* 2:11), that is, they have changed the worship of God into the traditions of men. What is it that lifts up one nation above another but the gospel? Above all nations of the earth, England has been lifted up to heaven.

5. When the gospel goes, all soul-happiness and blessedness goes. The gospel, you know, is the means appointed by God to bring souls to an acquaintance with Christ, to an acceptance of Christ, to an interest in Christ, to an assurance that he is theirs, and they are his. Now, when this goes, all soul-happiness and blessedness goes.

6. When the gospel goes, the special presence of God goes, for that still goes with the gospel. There is a general presence of God, as the psalmist speaks, 'Whither shall I go from thy spirit? or whither shall I flee from thy presence?' (*Psa.* 139:7). This presence of God reaches

[1] Eli's daughter-in-law spoke these words in naming Ichabod.

from heaven to hell; in that sense, God is included in no place and not excluded out of any place. But, alas! what is this general presence? When the gospel goes, the special presence of God goes. This leads me to the third question which is this:

Question III. Whether God will remove the gospel from England or no?

It is the fear of many; but I humbly suppose he will not.

Whatsoever darkness may be upon it, yet God will not remove it; and, if you please, I will offer a few things that indicate something, as to my own satisfaction, and, it may be, to yours also.

1. The rooting that it has got in the hearts of sinners and saints, in the judgments, affections, and consciences, both of sinners and saints. Certainly it has got so deep a root in the hearts of many thousands of saints and sinners, that it shall not be in the power of hell to raze it out.

2. The glorious anointings that are to be found upon many thousands of God's servants in this nation to preach the everlasting gospel, and who would be glad to preach upon the hardest terms, keeping God and a good conscience, to preach it freely, as the apostles of old did. And certainly God has not laid in this treasure that it should be turned into a heap of confusion, but that it should serve to the end for which he laid it in.

3. The ineffectiveness of all former attempts and designs to destroy the gospel. You know what endeavours of old there have been to darken this sun, to put

out the light of heaven, in the Marian days, and in other days since then; and yet it has defied prisons, racks, flames, pillories, or anything else to extinguish the glory of it.

4. All designs and attempts to extinguish the everlasting gospel have turned to the advancement, flourishing, and spreading of the gospel.

5. God never takes away the gospel from a people till the body of that people have thrust the everlasting gospel from them; when, indeed, they have been so bold as to thrust away the everlasting gospel, God has been severe unto them; but till the body of a people have thrust away the everlasting gospel, God has not taken it away from them. We see in 2 Chronicles 36:15-23, that although God sent his messengers early and late, they abused and slighted and scorned them, till there was no remedy. We have the same thing taught us in Jeremiah 25:1-14 and in Acts 13:45-47. Till the Jews came to thrust away the everlasting gospel, the Lord continued it to them.

6. The spreading of the everlasting gospel is the special means appointed by God for the destruction of antichrist. He is to be first consumed by the spirit of God's mouth and then destroyed by the brightness of his coming; the spirit of faith and prayer in them that would be willing to lay down anything rather than part with the gospel. God will not put his blessed church to the blush; he will not make them ashamed of their confidence.

7. Are there not multitudes of the children of believers who fall under many promises? And will not God make good his engagements to them? 'And the LORD thy God

will circumcise thine heart, and the heart of thy seed' (*Deut.* 30:6), 'The generation of the upright shall be blessed' (*Psa.* 112:2).

8. The strange and wonderful affections and tenderness that God has wrought in his children to the gospel; what meltings and mournings, and what a spirit of prayer has God put upon his people!

9. There are many young tender plants and buds of grace, such in whom the Spirit of God has stirred an hungering, thirsting, and longing after the great concerns of eternity.

I would, upon these grounds, with others of the like import, hope and believe that the Lord will not remove his everlasting gospel, however he may correct his people for their trifling with and slighting the glorious gospel. I have several times thought what a day of darkness was upon the world, in respect of sin and superstition. When Christ brought the everlasting gospel, what a day of darkness and superstition was on the whole earth! But you know what the apostle says, 'For after that in the wisdom of God the world by wisdom knew not God, it pleased God by the foolishness of preaching to save them that believe' (*1 Cor.* 1:21).

When it is nearest day, then it is darkest. There may be an hour of darkness that may be upon the gospel, as to its liberty, purity, and glory; and yet there may be a sunshining day ready to tread on the heels of it. And so much for the resolution of those questions.

I shall proceed, as I said, and leave some *legacies* with you, which may, by the finger of the Spirit, be made advantageous to you, when we are not at liberty to speak unto you.

1. The first legacy I would leave with you is this: Secure your interest in Christ; make it your great business, your work, your heaven, to secure your interest in Christ. This is not an age, an hour, for a man to be between fears and hopes, between doubting and believing.

Rest not in a name to live, when you are dead God-ward and Christ-ward; rest not in an outward form and outward privilege. They cried out, 'The temple of the LORD, the temple of the LORD,' that had no interest in, or love to, the Lord of the temple. Follow God, leave no means unattempted whereby your blessed interest may be cleared up.

2. Make Christ and Scripture the only foundation for your souls and faith to build on, as the apostle saith, 'Other foundation can no man lay than that is laid, which is Jesus Christ' (*1 Cor.* 3:11). 'Behold, I lay in Zion for a foundation a stone, a tried stone, a precious corner stone, a sure foundation' (*Isa.* 28:16). It is a very dangerous thing, as much as your souls and eternity is worth, for you to build on anything beside Jesus Christ. Many will say, Come, build on this authority and that, on this saying and that; but take heed.

3. In all places and company, be sure to carry your soul preservative with you. Go into no place or company, except you carry your soul preservations with you, that is, a holy care and wisdom. You know, in infectious times, men will carry outward preservatives with them; you had need to carry your preservatives about you, else

you will be in danger of being infected with the ill customs and vanities of the times wherein you live.

4. See that all within you rises higher and higher, by oppositions, threatenings and sufferings, that is, that your faith, your love, your courage, your zeal, your resolutions, and magnanimity rises higher by opposition and a spirit of prayer. Thus it did with the apostles (see *Acts* 4:18–21, 29–31). All their sufferings did but raise up a more noble spirit in them, they did but raise up their faith and courage. So in Acts 5:40–42, they looked on it as a grace to be disgraced for Christ, and as an honour to be dishonoured for him. They say, as David, 'If this be vile, I will yet be more vile.' If to be found in the way of my God, to act for my God, be vile, I will be more vile.

5. Take more pains and make more conscience of keeping yourselves from sin than suffering, from the pollutions and defilements of the day, than from the sufferings of the day. This legacy I would beg that you would consider; take more pains, and make more conscience of keeping yourselves from the evil of sin than the evil of punishment, from the pollutions and corruptions of the times than the sufferings of the times: 'Save yourselves from this untoward generation' (*Acts* 2:40). The children of God must be 'blameless and harmless . . . without rebuke, in the midst of a crooked and perverse nation' (*Phil.* 2:15). Hebrews 11 speaks full to the point in hand. Also Revelation 3:4 'Thou hast a few names even in Sardis which have not defiled their garments; and they shall walk with me in white: for they are worthy.' White was the habit of nobles, which imports the

honour that God will put on those that keep their garments pure in a defiling day. 'And I heard another voice from heaven, saying, Come out of her, my people, that ye be not partakers of her sins, and that ye receive not of her plagues' (*Rev.* 18:4). If you will be tasting and sipping at Babylon's cup, you must resolve to receive more or less of Babylon's plagues.

6. Be always doing or receiving good. Our Lord and Master went up and down in this world doing good; he was continually doing good to body and soul; he was acted by an untired power. Be always doing or receiving good. This will make your lives comfortable, your deaths happy, and your account glorious, in the great day of our Lord. Oh! how useless are many men in their generation! Oh! that our lips might be as so many honeycombs, that we might scatter knowledge!

7. Set before you the highest examples and patterns of grace and godliness for your imitation. In the business of faith, set an Abraham before your eyes; in the business of courage, set a Joshua; in the business of uprightness, set a Job; of meekness, a Moses. There is a disadvantage that redounds to Christians by looking more backwards than forwards. Men look on whom they excel, not on those they fall short of. Of all examples, set them before you that are most eminent for grace and holiness, for communion with God, and acting for God. Next to Christ, set the pattern of the choicest saints before you.

8. Hold fast your integrity, and rather let all go than let that go. A man had better let liberty, estate, relations,

and life go, than let his integrity go. Yea, let ordinances themselves go, when they cannot be held with the hand of integrity: 'God forbid that I should justify you till I die, I will not remove my integrity from me. My righteousness I hold fast, and I will not let it go: my heart shall not reproach me so long as I live' (*Job* 27:5-6). Look, as the drowning man holds fast that which is cast forth to save him, as the soldier holds fast his sword and buckler on which his life depends, so, says Job, 'I will hold fast my integrity; my heart shall not reproach me. I had rather all the world should reproach me, and my heart justify me, than that my heart should reproach me, and all the world justify me.' That man will make a sad exchange that shall exchange his integrity for any worldly concern. Integrity maintained in the soul will be a feast of fat things in the worst of days; but let a man lose his integrity, and it is not in the power of all the world to make a feast of fat things in that soul.

9. The ninth legacy that I would leave with you is this: Let not a day pass over your head without calling the whole man to an exact account. Where have you been acting today? Hands, what have you done for God today? Tongue, what have you spoken for God today? This will be an advantage to you in many ways—but I can only touch on these legacies.

10. Labour mightily for a healing spirit. This legacy I would leave with you as matter of great concern. Labour mightily for a healing spirit. Away with all discriminating names whatever that may hinder the applying of balm to heal your wounds. Labour for a healing spirit.

Discord and division become no Christian. For wolves to worry the lambs is no wonder, but for one lamb to worry another, this is unnatural and monstrous. God has made his wrath to smoke against us for the divisions and heart-burnings that have been amongst us. Labour for a oneness in love and affection with everyone that is one with Christ. Let their forms be what they will, that which wins most upon Christ's heart should win most upon ours, and that is his own grace and holiness. The question should be, What of the Father, what of the Son, what of the Spirit shines in this or that person? and accordingly let your love and your affections run out.

11. Be most in the spiritual exercises of religion. Improve this legacy, for much of the life and comfort, joy and peace of your souls is wrapped up in it. I say, be most in the spiritual exercises of religion. There are external exercises, as hearing, preaching, praying, and conference and there are the more spiritual exercises of religion, exercise of grace, meditation, self-judging, self-trial, and examination. Bodily exercise will profit nothing if abstracted from those more spiritual. The glory that God has and the comfort and advantage that will redound to your souls is mostly from the spiritual exercises of religion. How rare is it to find men in the work of meditation, of trial and examination, and of bringing home of truths to their own souls?

12. Take no truths upon trust, but all upon trial (see *1 Thess.* 5:21, *1 John* 4:1, *Acts* 17:11). It was the glory of that church, that they would not trust Paul himself—Paul, that had the advantage above all for external

qualifications—no, not Paul himself. Take no truth upon trust; bring them to the balance of the sanctuary. If they will not hold weight there, reject them.

13. The lesser and fewer opportunities and advantages you have in public to better and enrich your souls, the more abundantly address your souls to God in private: 'Then they that feared the LORD, spake often one to another' (*Mal.* 3:16, 17).

14. Walk in those ways that are directly cross and contrary to the vain, sinful, and superstitious ways which men of a formal, carnal, lukewarm spirit walk in; this is the great concern of Christians. But more of that by and by.

15. Look upon all the things of this world as you will look upon them when you come to die. At what a poor rate do men look on the things of this world when they come to die! What a low value do men set upon the pomp and glory of it, when there is but a step between them and eternity! Men may now put a mask upon them, but then they will appear in their own colours. Men would not venture the loss of such great things for them did they but look on them now, as they will do at the last day.

16. Never put off your conscience with any plea or with any argument that you dare not stand by in the great day of your account. It is dreadful to consider how many in these days put off their consciences. We did this and that for our families; they would have otherwise perished. I have complied thus, and wronged my conscience thus, for this and that concern. Will a man stand

by this argument when he comes before Jesus Christ at the last day? Because of the souls of men, many plead this or that. Christ does not stand in need of indirect ways to save souls; he has ways enough to bring in souls to himself.

17. Eye more, mind more, and lay to heart more the spiritual and eternal workings of God in your souls than the external providences of God in the world. Beloved, God looks that we should consider the operations of his hand; and the despising the works of his hands is so provoking to him that he threatens them to lead them into captivity for not considering them. But above all look to the work that God is carrying on in your souls. Not a soul but he is carrying on some work or other in it, either blinding or enlightening, bettering or worsening; and therefore look to what God is doing in your soul. All the motions of God within you are steps to eternity, and every soul shall be blessed or cursed, saved or lost to all eternity, not according to outward dispensations, but according to the inward operations of God in your souls. Observe what humbling work, reforming work, sanctifying work, he is about in your soul; what he is doing in that little world within you. If God should carry on never so glorious a work in the world, as a conquest of the nations to Christ, what would it advantage you if sin, Satan, and the world should triumph in your soul, and carry the day there.

18. Look as well on the bright side as on the dark side of the cloud; on the bright side of providence as well as on the dark side of providence. Beloved, there is a great

weakness amongst Christians; they do so pore on the dark side of the providence as that they have no heart to consider the bright side. If you look on the dark side of the providence of God to Joseph, how terrible and amazing was it! but if you look on the bright side, his fourscore years' reign, how glorious was it! If you look on the dark side of the providence of God to David, in his five years' banishment, much will arise to startle you; but if you turn to the bright side, his forty years' reign in glory, how amiable was it! Look on the dark side of the providence of God to Job, oh, how terrible was it in the first chapter of Job! but compare this with the last chapter, where you have the bright side of the cloud, and there God doubles all his mercies to him. Consider the patience of Job and the end that the Lord made with him. Do not remember the beginning only, for that was the dark side; but turn to the latter end of him, and there was his bright side. Many sins, many temptations, and much affliction would be prevented by Christians looking on the bright side of providence as well as on the dark.

19. Keep up precious thoughts of God under the sourest, sharpest, and severest dispensations of God to you: 'My God, my God, why hast thou forsaken me? why art thou so far from helping me, and from the words of my roaring? O my God, I cry in the daytime, but thou hearest not; and in the night season, and am not silent' (*Psa.* 22:1, 2). There was the psalmist under smart dispensations, but what precious thoughts he had of God after all: 'But thou art holy, O thou that inhabitest the praises

of Israel' (verse 3): though I am thus and thus afflicted, yet thou art holy. 'By terrible things in righteousness wilt thou answer us, O God of our salvation' (*Psa.* 65:5).

20. Hold on and hold out in the ways of well-doing, in the want of all outward encouragements, and in the face of all outward discouragements. It is nothing to hold out when we meet with nothing but encouragements; but to hold out in the face of all discouragements is a Christian duty: 'Though thou hast sore broken us in the place of dragons, and covered us with the shadow of death,' yet have we not 'dealt falsely in thy covenant: Our heart is not turned back, neither have our steps declined from thy way' (*Psa.* 44:17-19). It is perseverance that crowns all: 'Be thou faithful unto death, and I will give thee a crown of life' (*Rev.* 2:10); 'He that shall endure unto the end, the same shall be saved' (*Matt.* 24:13). It is perseverance in well-doing that crowns all our actions. If you have begun in the Spirit, do not end in the flesh; do not go away from the captain of your salvation; follow the Lamb, though others follow the beast and the false prophets.

21. In all your natural, civil, and religious actions, let divine glory still rest on your souls (*Rom.* 14:7, 8; *1 Cor.* 10:31). In all your bearings, in all your prayings, let the glory of Christ carry it; in all your closet duties, let the glory of Christ lie nearest your hearts.

22. Record all special favours, mercies, providences, and experiences. It is true that a man would do nothing else should he record all the favours and experiences of God towards him; and therefore my legacy is record all

special favours, peculiar experiences. Little do you know the advantage that will redound to your soul upon this account by recording all the experiences of the shinings of his face, of the leadings of his Spirit. Many a Christian loses much by neglecting this duty.

23. Never enter upon the trial of your estate but when your hearts are at the best and in the fittest temper. It is a great design of Satan, when the soul is deserted and strangely afflicted, to put the soul on trying work. Come, see what you are worth for another world, what you have to show for a better state, for an interest in Christ, a tide for heaven. This is not a time to be about this work. Your work is now to get off from this temptation, and therefore to pray and believe and wait upon God, and to be found in all those ways whereby you may get off the temptation.

24. Always make the Scripture, and not yourselves, nor your carnal reason, nor your bare opinion, the judges of your spiritual state and condition. I cannot see my condition to be good. I cannot perceive it. What! must your sense and your carnal reason be the judge of your spiritual state? 'To the law and to the testimony: if they speak not according to this word, it is because there is no light [no morning] in them' (*Isa*. 8:20). 'The word that I have spoken, the same shall judge [you] in the last day' (*John* 12:48). The Scripture is that which must determine the case in the great day, whether you have grace or no, or whether it be true or no.

25. Make much conscience of making good the terms on which you closed with Christ. You know the terms,

how that you would deny yourselves, take up your cross, and follow the Lamb wheresoever he should go. Now you are put to take up the cross, to deny yourselves, to follow the Lamb over hedge and ditch, through thick and thin. Do not turn your backs on Christ; the worst of Christ is better than the best of the world. Make conscience of making good your terms, to deny yourself, your natural self, your sinful self, your religious self to follow him; and if you do so, oh! what an honour will it be to Christ and advantage to your souls and a joy to the upright!

26. Walk by no rule but such as you dare die by and stand by in the great day of Jesus Christ. You may have many ways prescribed to worship by, but walk by none but such as you dare die by, and stand by, before Jesus Christ. Walk not by a multitude, for who dare stand by that rule when he comes to die?

Make not the example of great men a rule to go by, for who dare die by and stand by this in the great day of account? Do not make any authority that stands in opposition to the authority of Christ a rule to walk by, for who dare stand by this before Jesus Christ? Ah! sirs, walk by no rule but what you dare die by and stand by at the great day.

27. And lastly, sit down and rejoice with fear. Let the righteous rejoice, but let them 'rejoice with trembling' (*Psa.* 2:11). Rejoice, that God has done your souls good by the everlasting gospel; that he did not leave you till he brought you to an acceptance of, to a closing with, and a resignation of, your souls to Christ, and the clearing up

of your interest in him. Rejoice, that you have had the everlasting gospel in so much light, purity, power, and glory, as you have had for many years together. Rejoice in the riches of grace that has carried it in such a way towards you. And weep, that you have provoked God to take away the gospel, that you have no more improved it; that you have so neglected the seasons and opportunities of enriching your souls. When you should have come to church-fellowship, anything would turn you out of the way. Oh! sit down and tremble under your barrenness, under all your leanness. Notwithstanding all the cost and charge that God has been at, that you have grown no more into communion with God and conformity to God and into the lively hope of the everlasting fruition of God.

Here are your legacies, and the Lord make them to work in your souls, and then they will be of singular use to you, to preserve you so that you may give up your account before the great and glorious God with joy. Labour to make conscience of putting these legacies into practice, of sucking at these breasts, which will be of use to us, till we shall be gathered up into the fruition of God, where we shall need no more ordinances, no more preaching, no more praying.

JOHN COLLINS

LIFE

John Collins was born in England about 1632, but the exact date and place of his birth are as uncertain as most of the other details of his life. While he was still a child, his family emigrated to New England, where his father became a deacon of the church at Cambridge, Massachusetts, during the famous pastorate of Thomas Shepard. In his youth, John received a severe wound and lay, as he thought, dying, when Shepard came and assured him that he had been wrestling with God for his life, and had been granted his desire. Collins recovered and was educated at Harvard College, graduating in 1649. After a fellowship there, he returned to the land of his birth, where he spent the rest of his life. At the end of the Commonwealth period in 1659, he was Chaplain to General Monk and held no benefice at the time of the Ejection.

Some time after the Act of Uniformity, Collins became pastor of an Independent congregation at Paved Alley, Lime Street, which had been first gathered by Dr Thomas Goodwin. When, during the respite from persecution in 1672, the City merchants established a lecture at Pinner's

Hall, Collins was chosen to deliver this in rotation with five other distinguished Puritans—Bates, Manton, Owen, Baxter and Jenkyn—an indication of his own calibre as a preacher.

Collins, having remained inactive throughout the darkest years of the quarter-century of persecution since 1662, died in 1687 and was interred at Bunhill Fields. His son was an intimate friend of the commentator Matthew Henry. Though to posterity one of the more obscure Puritans, Collins was held in high esteem during his own lifetime for his gracious character and pastoral gifts.

CONTENDING FOR THE FAITH

Earnestly contend for the faith which was once delivered unto the saints.
Jude 3

These words contain two parts:

I. We should *retain the faith* delivered to the saints.

II. We should *earnestly contend* to keep it.

I. What is here meant by faith? It is not so much the grace of faith, but the doctrine of faith; not special faith, by which we apprehend special mercy upon a promise made to the elect, but the faith that is believed, the whole substance of the doctrine of Christ, as to things that are to be believed and duties that are to be practised.

But why is it said that the faith was *once* delivered? Because it has been given finally, irrevocably, once for all.

'Delivered to the saints,' respects the privilege the saints of God had in the faith that God had left them. It is the faith of the gospel, committed as a treasure to them. The church is called a candlestick, not only to hold out the light, but to hold the light; whence the church is called the pillar and ground of the truth. Not that the church is to make doctrines, but to hold forth the doctrines of Christ, even as tablets and pillars, upon which proclamations are hung and held forth to be made public. The church of Christ is that place in which the truths of the Lord Jesus are kept and will be kept from one age to another.

II. But what is the import of the word 'earnestly contend'? It is a word used only once in the New Testament. The root of the word is frequently used and imports a struggling with might and main, as is seen in those who run at games. It is used for Jesus Christ in his sufferings. He was in agony: the same word from whence this word is compounded. The apostle would imply such a contention, such a struggling to keep the faith of the gospel, that one word in the English is not able to express it, and interpreters very much differ as to what is the import. The best centre in this, that we should contend for the faith, as men that would contend to keep their very lives.

The proposition is this, that it is the duty of the saints of God to maintain an earnest contention, to struggle for, and to keep the faith that was entrusted with them. Wherein does this contention consist?

1. It is not a carnal contention. The weapons of our warfare are not carnal, but spiritual. The saints are not called to contend for the faith with carnal weapons, with carnal power and force. 'Not by might, nor by power, but by my Spirit, saith the LORD of hosts.' The use of

fleshly arm—prison, pillars, and chains, and the taking away of men's comforts and estates upon the account of the faith of the gospel—has been the usual way in which error has defended itself; but prayers and tears are the church's weapons.

2. It is not a contention of uncharitableness, for it allows no murdering, either of the bodies or souls of men. Christians are so to contend against error and sinful practices as to love men's persons and pity those they contend with. Some are of the opinion that there is no way to show a holy zeal against errors, nor is it possible to destroy them, except by a holy separating from the persons of those who hold them. There are some to whom it is not lawful to say God speed or receive them into our houses: but yet this is in order to the saving their souls: 'others save with fear, pulling them out of the fire' (*Jude* 23).

But positively this holy contention consists in these four things:

1. By a right management of the sword of the Spirit, the Word of God, against errors and sinful practices, to be able to confute them mightily, as Apollos did, out of the Scriptures, showing the Jews that Jesus is the Christ.

2. By prayer: to pray down sinful opinions and practices. Thus when we pray, 'Thy kingdom come,' we ask that the gospel may run and be glorified, that these nights of darkness may be dispelled, that truth may shine to the perfect day.

3. By holy practising against errors; by holding forth the word of life in your conduct; by striving together

by a mutual provocation for the faith of the gospel in respect of holy walking.

4. By being able to suffer for the sake of the truth.

I shall now sum up all in a word of exhortation. Let every one that bears the name of a saint take up this exhortation of the apostle, 'Earnestly contend for the faith that was once delivered to the saints.' The sum of all is: Be valiant for the truth of Christ. Whatever has been delivered to you consonant to the truth, agreeable to the faith delivered to us, struggle for with might and main, by all Christian courage, by argument, practice, prayer, by suffering, rather than let go those truths that God has taught you by his faithful ministers. That Christ who has been preached to you; those Scriptures you have in your hands; those doctrines you have learned by experience, by prayer, by searching the Word; those ways of worship God has taught you; those patterns of his house, and outgoings and returnings there, which he has taught you—hold them fast, and do not let them go. 'Contend earnestly for the faith.'

It is to be lamented that there is so sad a spirit of indifference among Christians at this present day. Many act as if there were nothing in the gospel of Christ that were worthy the owning by practising, or worthy the owning by suffering. This lukewarm, indifferent disposition has done the church of God a great deal of mischief formerly and, if admitted now, will do as much mischief again. It has been one of the sins that the Lord at this day is judging and punishing his poor people for. Our zeal has been so hot against one another for mere externals and so cold when we are like to lose the substance. Our contentions rise so high in matters hardly of any moment, and our spirits work so low when they are to gain the great things for which Christ suffered and which he delivered to us.

It is my work, therefore, to beg you that you would put on a holy resolution, that there may be no contention among us (for we are brethren) but only that contention which may most retain, and best give witness to, the faith that is delivered to us. It is a trust God has committed to us, and he expects us to manage it with courage and confidence, to keep the faith of the gospel. There are very great oppositions against you, and there ought to be great resolutions in Christians to maintain themselves against such oppositions. It is a very sad thing, if, when Christians see the faith and the way of the gospel of God, as it were, taken from them at any time, they have not one word to speak, nor anything at all to venture in suffering for the ways and truths of Jesus Christ. Moses had such a holy zeal that when Aaron was an example to the people to lead them to idolatry, he contended with him earnestly to his face. The zeal of God's servants is so small now, that though Balaam is attacking God's work, we have not a word to speak. Though the false prophets of antichrist are engaged about the business, yet no Christian has courage to speak. As for the holy apostle Paul, when Peter walked with an uneven foot and began to Judaize, he tells us that he resisted him to his face. Shall Paul resist Simon Peter, and shall not the saints of God resist Simon Magus? Shall they resist Hymenaeus and Philetus, and shall not we contend with Alexander the copper-smith? It is but what God expects; and the exhortation here given us is that we should maintain with might and main, as that which is our treasure, the faith once delivered to the saints.

To put you upon this, I might encourage you with several things. All the reasons mentioned are so many motives to this holy spiritual contention.

1. The mercy of God in delivering the truth to you should engage you to this holy contention. It is such a mercy as is a non-such mercy. 'He sheweth his word unto Jacob, his statutes and his judgments unto Israel. He hath not dealt so with any nation' (*Psa.* 147:19, 20). How many of those that we call Christians in the world, are put, like Samson, to grind among the Philistines! They are taken up with superstition, popery, idolatry, will-worship, such things as Jesus Christ never delivered to his saints, as if both their eyes were put out. The Scripture light that should have showed them the truth is taken from them. Their consciences that should teach them are carried in the pocket of some base priest, and they dare not believe any other than what he will tell them. How many there are, even of the very reformed of the world, who only get upon some broken plank of shipwreck truth, on which they swim to the Lord Jesus? But God does not deal thus with us. You have had the whole counsel of God revealed to you, a glorious light set up in the nation for a hundred years past, which has been like the light of seven days. For these twenty years past the running to and fro of men has increased knowledge. You have learned the truth

from God's faithful ministers. You have received it with much affliction, with many temptations. It has cost Jesus Christ dear to send it, it has cost you dear to receive it; and will you let it go? Your sin above all others will be most provoking to the Lord Jesus.

2. I might tell you that it is a time in which many let go the faith, and methinks the Lord Jesus does by his poor and unworthy messenger say to this great congregation, as once he did to his apostles, 'Will ye also go away?' There are many that have been forward and eminent professors of the faith delivered to the saints that have made shipwreck of faith and a good conscience. Will you split upon the same rock? God has kept the truth for you and kept you in the truth hitherto, and he is coming to see whether you will cleave to it and keep it or no. We have been sucking at the breasts of the ordinances and dandled upon the knees of providences and gone on in a smooth way of profession; but what will you do now, when you must come possibly to suffer persecution for it? To keep the faith, you may lose your liberty, your life, your estate. And there is a great deal of hazard upon this account, for it has pleased God so to dispose it, that those that should be your guides into truth, the Lord is removing them into corners. Possibly while they have been with you, you have kept the faith; but what will you do when they are gone? While Moses was with the people they cleaved to the Lord; when once he was gone into the mount, they fell into their idolatry and worshipped a calf. While Paul was at Ephesus the flock kept pure, but (saith he) 'I know

after my departure grievous wolves shall break in, not sparing the flock.'

So while you have heard of God, who sends voices and warnings to scare away the wolves and foxes from you, possibly you may keep the faith; but what will you do when God removes them?

3. God has ever had in all ages of his church, a word of his patience to be kept, to try his saints, and therefore it concerns you to be valiant for the truth. In all the series of God's dispensations with his church, there has been something or other of the faith of Christ, that has cost them resisting to blood, the sacrificing of their lives, the laying down of all that they have for it by suffering. Now even as they, so we; if not in the same thing, yet in the same faith. We have still some word or other of God's patience to keep, therefore we need to have on the armour of light. You must wrestle with the fiery trial. There is some jewel that Jesus Christ puts upon you to wear, that persecutors and persecutions, heresies and heretics, will scratch at, which you must hold out with loss of life to keep; and this must be till the latter part of the rage and reign of antichrist is over; and even as you keep that, so will God keep you (*Rev.* 3:10). As you honour the word of God's patience, so God will honour you. As you are faithful to him, so will he give you the crown, and no otherwise. Hence therefore it concerns us all to be armed with a holy confidence and resolution, as to this spiritual warfare, in contending for the faith delivered to us.

But the great thing I shall speak about is: How may

Christians be helped in this holy struggling and contention? I shall only mention five or six things, some to fit you for it, others to help you in the management of it.

Rule I. Bring all doctrines that are offered you to believe and all practices that are put upon you to practise to the test of the Scriptures, the Word of God. Try them there, whether they are to be retained or to be rejected. You will thus discover what is right and what is wrong; and you will have on the best part of your armour by which to contend against error.

You will discover what is right and what is wrong; for the Scripture alone is the touchstone of doctrines and the trial of spirits. The Scripture reveals itself and reveals all things that are contrary to it. When you are bidden to try all things, it is not by practising all things, as some poor giddy-headed Christians of late days have done, who have made the practising every opinion to be their trying of it till they have run themselves into all opinions. But it is the Scripture you are first to try and then to practise, like the noble Bereans, that were more noble than those of Thessalonica because they searched the Scriptures. Bring the truths that have or shall be taught you and the doctrines that shall be imposed upon you to the Word of God. See whether they be according to the truth or no: for false doctrines and false worship of all things hate the Scripture most. They are like false coin or false jewels, which go best in the night. False coin will not endure the touchstone, nor false jewels the day. No more will false doctrines the Scripture, therefore it will be a great way to discover them.

This will be a great way to vanquish them. Take 'the sword of the Spirit' (*Eph.* 6:17). The Word of God is the sword of the Spirit, by which we slay heretical doctrines and by which we are to slay sinful practices. All those stones that the Davids of God have flung at the Goliaths of error, they have been taken out of the brook of the Scriptures. Therefore reduce all doctrines offered you to believe, all kinds of worship that are taught you to practise, to the Word of God.

All doctrines that are taught you to believe, reduce them thither; there is no profession of faith to be built; but the stones must be fetched from this mountain. If you believe divine truths, but not because the Scripture propounds them, your faith is but human. If you believe anything the Scripture does not speak, your faith is diabolical. The Word of God and your faith must run parallel. All that is written you must believe, and you must believe nothing but what is written. This was the rule of the Old Testament: 'To the law and to the testimony' (*Isa.* 8:20); to the law, that is, to Moses; and to the testimony, that is, to the prophets; 'if they speak not according to this word . . . there is no light in them.' When anything was offered to Christ by way of enquiry, his common answer was, 'How readest thou?' (*Luke* 10:26). 'How is it written?' When the apostle Paul would correct the abuse of the Lord's supper, he does not carry the Corinthians to such and such fathers, to this and that tradition and custom, but brings before them how it was delivered from the Lord. He reduces them to the institution, 'What I have received from the

Lord, that have I delivered unto you.' The Word of God is perfect in respect of doctrine and in respect of worship, so that whatever is offered you to believe, you must try it by Scripture's perfect rules, for it is given by divine inspiration, to make the man of God perfect and wise unto salvation. It is such a canon about doctrines to be received, as nothing must be added to nor taken from it (*Rev.* 22:18). Therefore it is called a testament. Now no man dares add to another man's last will and testament. Who shall dare to add a faith to the faith of God's elect, to that which Christ has delivered? I will give you this as a most certain observation: that there never was anything of false doctrine brought into the church or anything of false worship imposed upon the church, but either it was by neglecting the Scripture or by introducing something above the Scripture.

Bring hither all practices of worship, as well as doctrine. Try the ways and forms of Christ's house by the Word of Christ. He shows us the pattern thereof, the outgoings and returnings thereof. He was faithful in all his house, even as Moses was, who did not omit a pin of the tabernacle, but did appoint it. There is nothing decent and comely in the church, which is so much pleaded for, but what comes in by Christ's institution. Whenever you worship without a warrant from the Word of God or by whatever means you worship without a warrant from the Word of God, you worship you know not what (*John* 4:22). It is will-worship, and by the rule by which you receive one form of will-worship, you may receive twenty. It is vain worship; it will never bring you into communion with God, for he is a Spirit and seeks spiritual worshippers. It will never bring you to the enjoyment of God. So I say again, bring all questions of worship to the Word of God. And as to faith and worship, say, Oh! my faith and my worship, hitherto shalt thou go and no further.

This rule, rightly improved, will disentangle you from the hooks and take you off from the baits of those cunning fowlers (for to such the apostle compares them in the New Testament) who seek to draw souls away from the simplicity of gospel-faith. To put up false doctrine, they put down the Scripture and put out the eyes of Christians to make them bend to it. Before they use other means to compel them, their great work is to darken the light, or the truth; and in the place of the Scripture they set up other rules. Of these, three are marvellously popular, and I will mention them to show their opposition to this rule I have given you.

There is a threefold rule men would set up to deceive poor souls—the name of the church; ancient customs; the general practice of those where they live.

The first means which men would set up as a rule of doctrine and worship is the specious name of the church. This was the plea of the popish party in the Marian days. What! will you not believe the church? Has not the church power to make institutions and canons about this and that and the other? Will you not believe the church? Will you go out from the true church? Thus do men act who go about to deceive. There's nothing like it! In the work of catching and deluding many poor souls, many evil ministers make the church their rule! It was the way of the popish party of old, and if antichrist ever has power again over the church of Christ in that measure and degree it has had, you must expect it again: therefore, let me caution you against it. Need we enquire who this church was? It was only the decree of the proud church, antichrist of old, and the antichristian clergy, who (as you may read in their stories) would lord it over the faith of God's heritage. I must tell you that the name and custom and way of the true churches of Christ is a reverend holy thing. It is a weighty argument when the apostle says, 'We have no such custom, nor the churches of Christ.' And therefore I fully agree with him who said: No sober man will go against reason. No Christian will go against the Scripture: and no peaceable-minded man will go against the church. But then the church must shine by a Scripture-light. If that be a rule, it must be ruled by the Scripture. The church's power is not authoritative, as to give laws against the laws of Christ: it is only ministerial. We believe the Scripture for itself, and not because of the church; we receive the Scripture by the church. Therefore, when we set up the name of a church, let us see whether that church walks in the way of Christ, whether she is his spouse or no, whether she acts according to his institutions, whether they bring his light, yea or no; then submit. For it is not what a church practises, but what it is warranted to practise: not what it holds for a truth, but what it is warranted to hold as the word of truth. The Word was written after the church; but as it is the Word of God, it is before it. This, therefore, will break the snare. If you be set upon by the specious name of the church, look that the church has warrant from Scripture-institution, and then submit to church-institution.

A second means I observe men would set up to draw poor souls away from the faith once delivered to them is ancient custom: 'Our fathers worshipped in this mountain.' When they would hold forth that which the Scripture is short in, they will send us to such and such customs of so many hundred years' standing. It is to be bewailed that the date and standing of false doctrines and false worships is so ancient; for though at first they were but innovations, yet to succeeding generations they become old. Now it is a very great truth that what is the most ancient is the most true; and therefore there lies a great snare in this. Therefore when antiquity is pretended, if you find not their hoary heads in the way of righteousness, there is little reason for you to reverence them or comply with them any more than there was reason so suddenly to be taken with the Gibeonites' mouldy bread and clouted shoes. When matters of antiquity are pretended, say as Ignatius did, 'Jesus Christ is my antiquity.' So say, truth is my antiquity: for though an opinion has been held a thousand years, yet men must have the Word of truth in their hearts that is more ancient than all.

A third guide that men would set up is the general practice of the world or the generality of those in the place where they live. This was what the popish party did often mention to the witnesses of Jesus Christ. What! will you be wiser than others? Cannot you do as others do? Must you be singular? This is a specious argument to make you yield to those things the Word of God will not warrant, if you bring not this matter to the Word of God. It is not what the most do, but what Scripture authorizes us to do. It is not what the practice of all in general is, but what ought to be the singular care and strict holiness of Christians in particular, that the Word of God will allow. Christians are not to be conformed to the present world (*Rom.* 12:2). The Word will tell you that it is no more safe to follow a multitude to do evil than it will be sweet to be in hell with a great company. The Word will let you know that the secrets of the Lord are with a very few, namely, with those that fear him. As for the whole world, it lies in wickedness. The Word will tell you that the way of Jesus Christ and the profession of Jesus Christ is commonly called a sect; it is everywhere spoken against, and men hate it everywhere. Therefore set up this Scripture rule in your hearts, in your houses, in your meditations, in your practice.

Rule II. Be very well rooted and established in the faith that has been delivered to you. I observe that one of the great reasons why Christians so easily let go the profession they have made is because they were never well built upon it nor established in it. There are many Christians that, through their own itching ears and the heaping up teachers to themselves, have never been rooted or established in the truth. The Lord pity them and keep them this day! Many Christians that have attended upon the means of grace, have never seriously considered nor laid things to their heart, but are like those the apostle speaks of in Hebrews 5:12, that had need to learn again the first principles of the oracles of God. How many there are among us who profess with the highest but have little ground for their faith! They rest, as did the Jews, on the traditions of the elders, the custom of the place, or mere education. They accept a teaching because such and such a party of men holds it, because nobody denies it, because ministers commonly preach it. But the solid and serious ground of faith they have yet to seek. It is not with the things of God as with other arts, as logic, rhetoric, and astronomy. In these arts the principle is presupposed to be proved. No man goes about to prove that there is reason, that there is number, that there are heavenly bodies, because sense and experience alike show it. But it is quite otherwise in the things of God, for you are not only to run away with the notion that there is a God, that this God is one, and that these are his words and his works; but you are to show this by experience, because the knowledge of these things comes by infusion, by faith, by a belief that God is, for 'through faith we understand that the worlds were framed by the word of God' (*Heb.* 11:3).

Therefore I would press you to labour for an established spirit. You must not only hear the things of God, but see them; the first will but blind you, or at best leave you in great uncertainty; the last will settle you. When the apostles were under the greatest threatenings of the high priests and were forbidden to speak in the name of

Christ, what was the reason of the holy apostles' zeal, in speaking of justification by faith and the resurrection of Christ from the dead and forgiveness of sins by him (things that are very remote from sense and reason)? The apostle will tell you in Acts 4:20: 'We cannot but speak the things which we have seen and heard.' Hence it is that poor simple women who, by reason of the infirmity of their sex and the terrors of the fire and faggot, might readily have been brought to apostacy, yet they confounded the great doctors and rabbis when they were brought before them. They were able to burn, though they could not dispute; they beheld things that were invisible. It is an excellent thing not to take up the Word upon notion, upon opinion, but to have an established heart through grace.

In order to have a heart established through grace, get the Lord himself by prayer to teach you every truth. What Jesus Christ teaches once is everlastingly taught; no word is abiding, but what the Lord Jesus teaches himself. See how it is with Satan; when he comes to seduce men from the truth, he presents such a fine notion without, and commonly he darts such a dazzling light within, that you never knew a heretic take up a false opinion, but it was with a marvellous deal of sweetness and comfort. So when the Lord Christ teaches by his Spirit, he comes with such light, sweetness, savour, and relish of truth, that it will be impossible for you to let it go. Hence when Christ would confute the Pharisees, who had the witness of his Father in his work, he says, 'Ye have neither heard his voice at any time, nor seen his shape' (*John* 5:37). It is an excellent thing to see the shape and hear the voice of God.

Again, be well rooted in Christ, or else you will never be established in any truth of Christ. If you miss the Lord Jesus by the grace of faith, you will never hold fast the doctrine of faith. You are built upon the doctrine of the apostles (not their persons), the Lord Jesus being the cornerstone. He that does not know Jesus Christ himself will certainly lose his faith. What is the reason the stony-ground hearers in time of persecution fell away? Why, they had no root; they were not planted upon the Lord Jesus.

Rule III. Those truths that God has taught you, and those ways of worship God has committed to you, love them as your lives, love them above your lives; for no man will ever contend to hold them if he does not love them. Things of low price and esteem are soon let go. He that loves the Word above his life will let life go rather than the Word. If you receive not the Word out of love, every imposter and false prophet, every fear and terror of men, will rob you of it. Hide the Word in thy heart, says Solomon, love the truth dearly. It was a great saying of Calvin: 'Never did anyone apostatize from the truth of Jesus Christ, but it was because he did not love the truth.' And I add this, that never did any apostatize from the ways and truths of Jesus Christ, but it was because they did not receive them in love, or else they have lost their love, for there is a decay of affection as well as having no affection. If you love them, what will you not suffer for them? But more of that by and by.

Rule IV. Guard all the truths of God, and those ways of God that have been taught you; guard them strongly, especially truths that are most material and fundamental. For leading truths are like captains of armies, if they be routed, the rout of the whole follows. There is great opposition that will be made against your faith. The whole power of darkness, of antichrist, of his seducing spirits, likely and probably enough will overspread the whole face of Christendom once more. For she must sit as a lady before she be desolate and forsaken for ever. The apostle bids you beware of dogs; beware of the concision; beware of evil workers; guard yourselves against them. Guard the truths you have learned, by argument, by Scripture, by reason, that you may have wherewithal to confute them by the Word of truth mightily, out of the Scripture, as the apostle did.

Three things you are to guard against. The first is your own deceitfulness, especially in a rash and sudden forsaking of those ways that you have been taught and the profession you have taken up. Christians would never be so mad as to apostatize were they but seriously to deliberate about the weight of them, 'O foolish Galatians, who hath bewitched you, that you should not obey the truth?' *etc.* (*Gal.* 3:1), and 'I marvel that you are so soon turned away to another gospel' (*Gal.* 1:6). One would have thought they might have spoken with Paul first and sent to him and reasoned the case with him. There is a marvellous bewitching in false doctrines to take men suddenly who are not watchful over themselves. It is in disputations and practising truth, as it is in contentions.

If you form a judgment before you hear both parties speak, you judge unrighteously. If you forsake the ways and truths of Jesus Christ before you can hear what can be said for them, you act unrighteously.

The second thing to guard against is the lusts of your own hearts. The great work of a Christian is contention; it is not so much against antichrist, those that are without him, as that which is within him. If all heretical doctrines and ways and the memory of them were rooted out of the world, the heart is bad enough in one day to set them all on foot again; therefore guard the truth. Men of corrupt minds will soon grow reprobate as to the faith (2 *Tim.* 3:8). Such doctrines and worships as shall suit with our lusts, as shall suit with exalting self and laying Christ low, as shall suit with an easy way to heaven (when the Scripture says, 'Strait is the gate'), as shall suit with self-preservation and the preservation of my estate and liberty—I would suspect such doctrines as these before I take them up as the ways of Christ.

The third thing to guard the truth against is false teachers. Such come among you in sheep's clothing yet are wolves at heart. They creep in at unawares among you to subvert souls. I will not here describe them, for you know them well enough by their fruits. Only let me tell you in opposition to those; though you cannot attend upon the public ministry of the Word or upon those whom God has set over you, yet be diligent to take defences from them, as you may by their counsel, prayer, help and assistance, to guard you against false teachers. When the church of Christ is in the wilderness, you will find this is what the Holy Ghost advises them to do (*Song of Sol.* 1:8). You are to guard yourselves by communion one with another and to go forth by the footsteps of the flock. Also you are to go and feed your kids by the shepherds' tents, for though it is not the work God calls for, to pin your faith upon their sleeves, yet it is your duty to enquire of the Lord by them, for they are the messengers of the Lord to you.

Rule V. Arm yourselves with resolution to suffer for the faith of the gospel and for the ways of Jesus Christ. As you should love the truth above your lives, so labour to be made willing to part with life, estate, liberty, anything to keep the ways of Jesus Christ. It is not to the honour of the gospel of Christ to hear Christians break out into murmurings, passions, discontents, and contentions that are carnal and sinful. Your work is humbly, meekly, and patiently to lie under the hand of God and under the hand of man too; that is becoming to Christians. Suffering is that which will restore the glory of religion, will keep the truth delivered to you, and will honour the cause of Christ best of all. Follow the example of blessed Paul. His expression is worthy of consideration. In 2 Timothy 2:8, 9, he gives Timothy a charge to keep and propagate one of the most glorious truths, that Jesus Christ was risen from the dead, a truth that is farthest off from sense and reason, and he adds, 'wherein I suffer trouble.' Mark, Paul does not say, 'Wherein I make trouble,' but 'wherein I suffer trouble, as an evil doer, even unto bonds, but the word of

God is not bound.' If this blessed and glorious apostle would have had the faith of God bound and have contented himself with sinful silence and not propagated the gospel, Paul might have been free; but Paul would not have the Word of God bound, therefore Paul would suffer for it.

Shall we go a great deal higher than this? You have the glorious commendation of the Lord Jesus Christ upon this account, that he gave a free and full account of the doctrine of his Father, and of his glorious person, before Pontius Pilate, a bloody persecutor. It was not by bidding his disciples fight, but he gave a glorious confession before the face of Pilate, of the righteousness of his truth, doctrine, gospel, and of his person. Fear to ensnare the freedom of the truth with your own liberty; do not ensnare it to your own lusts, nor to the will of any man. Oh! that we could study and improve these Scriptures more! It would make us fear God more, and man less. It would make us say with holy David, 'Princes have persecuted me without a cause: but my heart standeth in awe of thy word' (*Psa.* 119:161). It is folly for a Christian to believe any doctrine or practise any worship for fear of man, who has no more power to hurt us than we give him ourselves by our fear. 'Fear not them which kill the body.'

It was the way of God's people formerly, that they learned to distinguish between duty commanded by God and that commanded by man. You may read how in all the days of antichrist's persecution, they came to distinguish between obedience to God and his truth and worship and obedience to man. Christians! nothing but a suffering spirit will help you to this, for there is no other way of obedience in this case to authority, but to suffer under it meekly, patiently, as lambs. This made the three children to divide between the command of the king and the command of God. What says Nebuchadnezzar? 'Every knee that bows not, shall be cast into the furnace.' 'As for that matter,' say they, 'O king, we are not careful to answer thee; for we will not bow down.' What, will they not obey him? Yes, they will obey him, by suffering, as becomes believers, and after the example of Christ. It is as if they should say, Truly we are terrified with the burning furnace, but we are terrified with hell too. We are terrified by your threats, O king, but we are likewise terrified with the threats of the great God. He is able to deliver us out of your torments; you are not able to deliver us from his torments. So was it in the case of Daniel.

Arm yourselves therefore with this resolution of suffering, and lie down patiently and meekly under those things that you cannot do, so that God may be honoured by your holy resolution upon this account. For truly, you never do contend successfully for the faith of the gospel, till you contend by suffering, for it is said, 'They overcome by the blood of the Lamb.' You never make religion your business till the world sees you can let such great things go as life, estate, and liberty, to keep it. Then wisdom is justified of her children. You never glorified the truths of God so much by practice or writing as by suffering for them. Those glorious truths against popish justification, the mixing of works with faith, transubstantiation, purgatory, idol-worship, against all those things that were superadded contrary to God's institution—there is such a glory upon these Reformation truths that it is hard for the popish power ever to darken them again because we see them written in the honourable and blessed scars of the witnesses and in the burnings of our glorious martyrs. When God takes away our faithful guides, take one another by the hand and say, Brethren, sisters, friends, come let us hold together. There is no way in the world to hold on together like suffering, for the gospel really gets more advantage by the holy, humble, sufferings of one gracious saint, simply for the word of righteousness, than by ten thousand arguments used against heretics and false worship. Compare Philippians 1:12-14 with verses 27-29. How are Paul's bonds a furtherance of the gospel? Paul no doubt was called an evil doer, one who sowed heresy and was hated everywhere. He says, 'many of the brethren in the Lord, waxing confident by my bonds, are much more bold to speak the word without fear.' Here is the great encouragement. In the 27th verse—and he speaks it as one that was leaving them—he says,

> Only let your conversation be as it becometh the gospel of Christ . . . that ye stand fast in one spirit, with one mind striving together for the faith of the gospel: And in nothing terrified by your adversaries . . . for unto you it is given in the behalf of Christ, not only to believe on him, but also to suffer for his sake.

It is given to you as a duty, given to you as a privilege.

Oh, that you would confirm one another and in slippery times hold up one another by the hand! Do it in obedience to God's call, in this way suffering for those truths you cannot otherwise hold and maintain.

Truly, Christians, you had need be armed with resolution, for the world is always counting for very little the things God's people have suffered, and they count it prudence not to meddle therein. Some who profess Christ's name are for easy and soft compliance, as if Christ gave them leave to agree to anything. I believe that some Christians are of the opinion that the saints of God are ill-advised to venture their all upon those truths they see others died and suffered for.

It is a sad thing, many Christians study to draw out the lines of obedience as far as the honesty of the times will give them leave, but no farther. They would go on with the Lord Jesus to the high priest's hall, and there deny him. They are willing, they say, to do anything for Christ, but they are willing to suffer nothing for Christ. To all such I say, you do very little honour Jesus Christ in this, and you will very little honour yourselves at the last. It is upon this account that some Christians, if they see, even against plain conviction of conscience and the Word, that there are superinstituted things broken in, such as in conscience they cannot submit to, yet they can comply. Why? They reply that they may be used lawfully, though not superstitiously. But the Apostle Paul says, 'Do I yet strive to please men?' (*Gal.* 1:10). 'Am I then the servant of Christ?' You cannot be the servants of Christ if you strive to please men. Woe be to you that please men and displease God. 'He that would be my disciple, let him deny himself, and take up his cross.' What is that? Deny wife, children, relations, comforts—he must be willing to forsake all. Those duties in which the Lord Jesus Christ is most glorified are either those our slothful hearts are most unwilling to do or those our fearful hearts are most unwilling to suffer for. Therefore arm yourselves with resolutions to suffer.

There are four appearances and coverings that saints usually take up to hide themselves, as under a covert, so as to evade the gospel-warrants, and the Lord's commands to suffer for the faith delivered.

The first is the notion that to a Christian there are things which are indifferent, mere toys and trifles, which they may do or may not do. It is not my work to tell you what is indifferent or name anything in particular. As I remember in the *Book of Martyrs*, the usual argument was, Why cannot you worship the idol? Why cannot you bow down as well as others? It is a small matter. Cannot you show your outward reverence, and keep your heart to yourself? Indeed if there were anything that is indifferent, a Christian has a marvellous latitude in point of doctrine and in point of worship. I would caution you therefore. The term *indifferent*, I suppose, is devised as a pillar to rest the conscience on, which otherwise would be startled. Things that come under this notion had need well to be weighed and considered. If they told you plainly that they came out of Rome and had the plague of popery upon them, that they came from hell, were hatched there, and that the curse of God was upon them, nobody would entertain them. They must pretend they came from the church, from the apostles, descending from the Scriptures; and hence they are entertained with such freedom and willingness that most Christians take no notice, but fall down under them; and so the very power and life of religion and holy practice is eaten out. The devil has three ways by which he makes men seek after him. First, commonly he covers holiness with other names. Secondly, he persuades men that sins are but little. Thirdly, that they may be repented of hereafter. The first is suitable to my purpose, that virtue or grace is covered with other names. If a man is holy, he is called precise; if zealous, he is said to be rash; and if it is really a sin, it shall come under the name of indifference, a toy, a trifle, and things of that nature. Therefore you had need be cautious, for it is not so much what name the sin has or what title it goes under, as what it is really. As to things of doctrine and worship, every man must give an account to the Lord of what he does; therefore I do not tell you what is indifferent and what not; but search the Scripture, and take heed what you receive as indifferent.

The second thing Christians will say, is, I hope I may comply with these things without danger, seeing that I bear them as my burdens. This is very much like the young man in the gospel; he came to Christ and would have him come up to his terms, and when Christ told him that yet he lacked one thing and must go and sell all, he went away sorrowful. Likewise, many Christians would follow Christ, but they cannot because there is not such security in it, so they go away sorrowful. You hypocrites! are you willing to forsake all for Christ, yet cannot leave life, liberty, and some of these small things? Will you wound the name of Christ and pretend to be sorrowful for it? Your pretence shall not excuse you; for so was Pilate loth to crucify Christ; and, as a means and expedient, he calls for water and washes his hands, saying, 'I am innocent from the blood of this just man.' But do you think God excused Pilate? No more will he you. Whatever is brought to you is either forbidden or commanded by God. If forbidden by God, why do you meddle with it? If commanded of the Lord, why are you burdened with it? Why do you do it heavily? For the Lord loves one that is cheerful in his service. Neither man nor God is pleased with such.

A third thing which satisfies many is that they may follow in some things the opinions of wise men, holy men, and good men; that they may do as they do. I shall say but these two words: first, many men are reputed good, wise, and honest, that are not so. A man may be accounted an honest man who yet may be covetous. He may be accounted a very good man, yet be really corrupt in heart and in his lusts. Therefore it is good to try men. I dare not trust mine own heart (unless God gives strength, grace, and assistance every moment) lest I should betray the truth of Christ for some worldly advantage. When the devil would set abroad an evil opinion or practice, it is his common way to present it to view in some clean vessel, in men of civil honesty and goodness. You read how the old prophet drew the young one in, though expressly forbidden of God himself (*1 Kings* 13:11-19). It may be the example of an old minister shall draw you: therefore it is good to mind whom you follow. Secondly, granted that they are all good and real, that they are men fearing God (as there are some), yet God will not let his people know all his mind. There are some that would, but cannot know all his mind and will. The Lord is free and sovereign; he reveals things necessary to salvation; but other things he may withhold. But what is your rule? Call no man master. You are to follow no man further than he follows Christ. Indeed for a man to follow the examples of others, who sin and do not know it, it is just like the case of holy Noah (who was a gracious man) who knew not the strength of the grape and was drunk with his own vineyards. But what was the fruit of it? His son Ham saw his nakedness and made it known. If good and holy men taste of the intoxicated wine that is too strong for them, and know it not, will you sip after them? If you do, you will display your nakedness and proclaim it from generation to generation; you will make yourselves Hams, not sons of the prophet. I know not what warrant you have to follow such examples.

The fourth thing which some Christians say is that it does no good by standing out. I answer, whether we get good, or do good, or no, we are to do our duty. The Lord will honour you for suffering for the truth (2 *Thess.* 1:2-5). And by suffering you shall confirm the saints and bear testimony; you shall witness against all false doctrines and false worship before the whole world. By your humility and patience, when you suffer not as evildoers, but as those that suffer for the Word of righteousness, the Word of truth, for holding fast the Lord Jesus and his faith—that is more precious than heaven and earth, than any created thing. This will make your name a sweet savour to all generations. As for those that apostatize, persecute, and oppose Jesus Christ, their memories shall be left as a curse to the people of God.

THOMAS LYE

LIFE

Thomas Lye was born at Chard, Somerset, in 1621. He entered Wadham College, Oxford, in 1636, but, after taking his Bachelor's degree, moved to Cambridge to continue his studies when Oxford became the head-quarters of the Royalists in the Civil War. He taught at Bury St Edmunds School for a short time, before returning to his native Chard as vicar. A supporter of the Westminster Confession of Faith, Lye, with many Presbyterian ministers, refused to take the Engagement in 1651 and was suspended from the ministry for a few months. He moved to London in 1657 when he became incumbent at All Hallows, Lombard Street, and remained here until the Ejection. Both in Somerset and London, he served on the Commission for the trial of ministers.

After 1662, Lye was an active conventicler[1] in London, preaching at Morgan's Lane, Southwark, and in his own house at Clapham, where he kept a school.

[1] That is, one who attended a 'conventicle,' a secret or illegal religious meeting, as was every Nonconformist gathering after the Act of Uniformity.—P.

More than once, he was in trouble with the authorities for his Nonconformity, for a time being imprisoned in Marshalsea. Lye was specially renowned as an instructor of children and had a great fondness for this work. He taught the catechism regularly on Saturday afternoons at Dyer's Hall and did not hesitate to use unusual methods to impress the truth upon his young hearers. Many of these remembered his labours with gratitude in after life, among them Edmund Calamy, the historian. Lye died and was buried at Clapham in June 1684. His published works include a number of sermons and some catechetical writings.

A PASTOR'S LOVE FOR HIS PEOPLE

Therefore, my brethren dearly beloved and longed for, my joy and crown, so stand fast in the Lord, my dearly beloved.
Philippians 4:1

My beloved, I do very well remember that upon the 24th of this month of August, in 1651, I was under the sentence of banishment; and that very day I preached my farewell sermon to my people from whom I was banished because I would not swear against my king, having sworn to maintain his just power and honour and greatness. And now behold a second trial! Then I could not forswear myself; the God of heaven keep me that I never may!

I am apt to think I could do anything for this loving congregation, only I cannot sin. But since, beloved, the sentence has gone out against us that we that cannot subscribe must not subsist, this is the last day that is prefixed to us to preach. I shall now speak to you (God assisting me), if my passions will give me leave, just as if I would speak if I were immediately to die. Therefore hearken, 'my brethren, dearly beloved and longed for, my joy and crown, so stand fast in the Lord, my dearly beloved.'

Paul was now a prisoner at Rome for the gospel of Christ. It was his second imprisonment, and he was not far from being offered up as a sacrifice for the *gospel* he had preached. This gospel the Philippians had heard him preach, and the godly Philippians, having heard of his imprisonment, sent so far from Philippi to Rome to visit him and to supply his wants. This was a gracious disposition, which I hope the eternal God has given the saints in London also, and for which, if for anything, God has a blessing in store for them. Paul is not so much concerned about his own bonds, as about the Philippians' state. Epaphroditus tells him that there were heresies and false doctrines got in amongst them, but yet the Philippians stood fast. In this Paul rejoices, writes this epistle, bids them go on, stand fast, keep their ground, and to be sure not to give an inch, but to stand fast, knowing that in the long run their labour would not be in vain in the Lord.

I shall without any more ado enter upon the text, in which you have two principal things.

I. A melting appellation: 'my brethren, dearly beloved and longed for.'

II. A serious exhortation: 'so stand fast in the Lord.' First, the matter of the duty: *stand*, stand it out, stand fast. Secondly, the manner of the duty: *so* stand: as you have stood, so stand fast. Stand fast *in the Lord*; stand so, stand in the Lord, in the Lord's strength, and in the

Lord's cause. To stand in your own strength would be the ready way to fall; and to stand in your own cause, for your own fancy, would be the ready way to expose yourselves to all manner of temptations. 'Therefore, my brethren, dearly beloved and longed for, stand, and so stand fast in the Lord, my dearly beloved.'

If there are any wicked catchers here, let them know that I shall speak no more than I shall draw from and is the mind of my text; I would not give occasion to be a greater sufferer than I am likely to be. But let me come to the words—

I. The melting appellation, 'my brethren, my dearly beloved.' Paul was an apostle and a high officer in the church of God, and he wrote to the Philippians, to all the Philippians, to the poorest of them; and see how he speaks to them—'my brethren.' Hence observe that the highest officers in the church of Christ, though they are indeed by office rulers over them, yet by relation they are no more than brethren to the meanest saint. Here we have no rabbis to whom we must bow because they say we must bow. Paul calls them brethren and so writes to them (cf. *Gal.* 1:2). Likewise James, a scriptural officer, one of the highest apostles Christ ever made, says, 'Hearken, my beloved brethren' (*James* 2:5). So, too, does Peter, an apostle of Christ: 'Wherefore the rather, brethren' (2 *Pet.* 1:10), and John, the beloved disciple, 'Brethren, I write no new commandment unto you' (*1 John* 2:7).

If then the highest officers in the church, such as Christ approves of, are but brethren to the meanest saint, then certainly they are but brethren to their fellow officers.

If there are any of a light spirit that would bear rule, and that love to have pre-eminence, I would desire them to read two Scriptures—Luke 22:25, 26 and Matthew 20:26-28. Does Christ say, 'Whosoever will be chief among you, let him be one that will domineer over your estates, over your persons, over your consciences?' No, 'but let him be your minister'—'let him be your servant, even as the Son of man came not to be ministered unto, but to minister, and to give his life a ransom for many.' You have this also in Luke 22:25, 26:

> And he said unto them, The kings of the Gentiles exercise lordship over them [i.e. over their slaves, over their vassals] . . . but ye shall not be so: but he that is greatest among you, let him be as the younger; and he that is chief as he that doth serve.

Surely, if Paul is but a brother to Philip, then he is no more to Timothy.

If the highest officers in the church of Christ are but brethren to the meanest saint, then it is not for those brethren to lord it over their fellow brethren. They are not to lord it over God's heritage—remember, it is God's heritage. I hope your consciences will bear me witness that I have laboured, as much as in me lies, to be a helper of your joy, not to lord it over your faith (2 *Cor.* 1:24), nor to press or cause you to believe this or that simply because I believe it. If this be allowed, then I may turn Papist tomorrow! Christ said to him that would have had him speak to his brother to divide the inheritance with him, 'Man, who made me a judge over you?' (*Luke*

12:14). So say I, Man, who made you a tyrant and lord over your fellow brethren? 'Neither as being lords over God's heritage' (*1 Pet.* 5:3).

If the highest officers in the church of Christ are but brethren, and no more, then there should be no discord between those brethren. 'Behold, how good and how pleasant it is for brethren to dwell together in unity'; and truly I may comfortably speak that, and it is one of the greatest comforts I have in the world. I hope we have lived together in love, blessed by God. Let us not fall out, for we are brethren. Beloved, the discords between pastor and people have made the best music in the ears of the Jesuits.

Are pastors, nay, the highest officers that Jesus Christ has and owns in the church, but brethren? Oh! then let those brethren, if they will appear before the bar of their Father in heaven with comfort, beware of offending the souls of their brethren; for at the hand of every brother God will require the soul of his brother. 'His blood will I require at the watchman's hand' (*Ezek.* 33:6). We that are called by some the dogs of the flock, shall we prove dumb dogs? What a comfort it will be to my dying brethren this day, if they can but say, Lord, we are clear from the blood of our brethren. The officers of Christ should so behave themselves as to never give their people occasion to say, We are brethren to dragons. But 'take ye heed everyone of his neighbour, and trust ye not in any brother' (*Jer.* 9:4). I would commend one Scripture to all my brethren in the ministry—1 Corinthians 8:13. It is a Scripture that I would have written in letters of gold on the lintel posts of all ministers' doors: 'Wherefore, if meat make my brother to offend, I will eat no flesh while the world standeth, lest I make my brother to offend.' Rather than endanger my soul, I'll away with all these toys and gew-gaws.[1] From the terms of dearest affection, 'dearly beloved and longed for,' observe that it becomes the highest ministers, much more the lowest, to bear a most tender, vehement, ardent, strong, melting affection towards that flock or people that God has committed to their charge. Thus Paul to the Philippians in the text: 'my brethren, dearly beloved and longed for.' You find Paul in all his epistles, in a thawing frame to his people, melting in love unto them. The Corinthians were so in his heart, not only to live with them but, if God called him, to die for them; so abundantly did he love them that he would very gladly spend and be spent for them (2 *Cor.* 12:15). He carried them in his heart and earnestly longed after them all. As for the Thessalonians, as a nurse he tends and nourishes them as children and is so affectionately desirous of them that he is willing to impart to them not only the gospel, but his own soul, because they were dear to him (*1 Thess.* 2:8).

Is this so? Ought pastors so to love their people? Give me leave to speak to you in the words of Job, in respect of those hundreds of ministers that are to be plucked from their people: 'Have pity upon me, have pity upon me, O ye my friends; for the hand of God hath touched me' (*Job* 19:21). What, will nothing serve but plucking out our very heart? How sad is it for the father to be

[1] Gaudy playthings, baubles.

plucked from the child, the shepherd from the flock, the nurse from the child! 'This is a lamentation, and shall be for a lamentation.' There must be a parting between David and Jonathan, who loved one another as their own souls. This cut them to their very heart, and this I may say, in respect to myself. I bless God that I cannot say, as she of her husband, 'a bloody husband hast thou been unto me,' but a loving congregation have you been unto me. I know that none of you have desired my destruction nor to taint my name. Never did I hear of three in this congregation speak of pressing anything against me that was contrary to my conscience; nor can I say that there are four in this parish that did ever refuse to pay me my legal due. Blessed be God for such a people! You have not encroached upon my conscience, as I hope I have not upon yours. Pastors must love their people; do not blame them if their hearts are almost broken, when they are to part from such a people.

Must the pastor love his people? Then the people must love their pastor. It is true that it lies in the power of man to separate pastor and people, but not to separate their hearts. I hope there will never be a separation of love, but that our love will still continue. If we do not see one another, yet we may love one another, and pray for one another. I hope a husband does not cease from loving his wife because she is absent from him. But, oh! for my brethren, hundreds of them think that you are undone; but you are not undone. Though you cannot see as far as other men, you may live in love and keep your conscience quiet.

Must pastors love their people? Then you may see from hence what should be the grand object of the pastor's affection, namely, the people, not what the people have. This is all too often the great inquiry: What is the benefice worth? What is the preferment? Do they pay well? Whereas we should not seek so much the fleece as the flock. We should not take oversight of a congregation for love of their pay, but of their souls. We should not say: It is an excellent good living, or as one I have heard of said, Let me have their tithes, and let their souls go to the devil. But we should say as the apostle, 'I seek not yours, but you' (2 *Cor.* 12:14). And I hope there may be many hundreds who can say that it has been the people's souls they have more loved and desired than anything that the people had.

Once more I say, We must love them, and love them tenderly. Yes, my beloved, we are so to love our people as to venture anything for them, except our own damnation. I come not here to throw firebrands. I bless God I have a most tender affection for all my brethren in the ministry; and though I am not satisfied with myself, yet I condemn no man. I believe that many of them do as conscientiously subscribe as refuse to subscribe. I protest in the fear of God, I cannot subscribe. Perhaps it is because I have not as much light as others have; for he that doubts, says the apostle, is damned. My beloved, I hope you would not have us sin against God and our own consciences. It is not my living that I desire, but my office to serve my Lord and Master. But if we should, to keep communion with you, lose our communion with

God, this is the ready way to have all our labour and pains lost; but as David said to Zadok (and, oh, that I could speak it with as good hopes as David!) 'Carry back the ark of God into the city: if I shall find favour in the eyes of the LORD, he will bring me again, and show me both it, and his habitation' (2 *Sam.* 15:25). Brethren, I could do very much for the love I bear to you, but I dare not sin. I know they will tell you that this is pride and peevishness in us, and that we are tender of our reputation, and we would fain all be bishops and forty things more; but the Lord be witness between them and us in this. Beloved, I prefer my wife and children before a blast of air of people's talk. I am very sensible of what it is to be reduced to a morsel of bread. Let the God of heaven and earth do what he will with me. If I could have subscribed with a good conscience, I would; I would do anything to keep myself in the work of God, but to sin against my God I dare not.

'My dearly beloved and longed for, my joy and crown'—my present joy and future crown! my joy which I value more than a crown, my principal joy! Hence observe that the fixed standing, and flourishing growth of the saints in gospel practice and gospel obedience, is, or ought to be, matter of transcendent joy to their pastors. It was so to the Apostle Paul. Paul heard how they stood. Though there was a plague amongst them, yet they were not infected; and though he was in gaol ready to be beheaded, yet this was his joy and crown that his people did stand. And I hope, my brethren, it will be our joy and crown to hear of your standing and growth in gospel-knowledge and profession so that, as John said: 'I rejoiced greatly, that I found of thy children walking in truth' (2 *John* 4).

It should be the prayers and endeavours of all pastors really to love the souls of their people and to pray for them that when they cannot look after the souls of their children, yet good nurses may be procured for them. What a joy it was that Moses' mother was made his nurse? and who can tell, it may be, though not because of any merit of ours, yet of their own clemency, our governors may give us to be nurses over our own children. But if I cannot nurse my child myself, I will wish it well, and as good a nurse as possible. Far be it for me to hope that those that are to take my place should not prosper. Lord, it shall be the prayer of thy servant that those that are to follow may have a double and treble portion of thy spirit, that they may be both painstaking and faithful and successful.

If the people's growth in grace and knowledge is matter of joy to a faithful pastor, then what do you think of those that hinder their thriving? I shall give you two Scriptures: 'The Pharisees therefore said among themselves' (they durst not speak it publicly; but whom was it against? Why, it was against Christ) 'Perceive ye how ye prevail nothing? Behold the world is gone after him' (*John* 12:19). They as much as said, We will lessen his congregation; if we cannot do that, we will shut the doors against him. 'Woe unto you, scribes and Pharisees, hypocrites! for ye shut up the kingdom of heaven against men' (*Matt.* 23:13). What! shut up the kingdom of heaven against men! What! the Pharisees, that pretended to have the keys of heaven, and to be the guides! Is it because there is not room enough in heaven for us and them too? No, for, Christ says, 'Ye neither go in yourselves, neither suffer ye them that are entering to go in.' I dare not tell you at this time what it is to shut up the kingdom of heaven against men. You may better imagine it than I can speak it; but this is what the Pharisees did; they would not go in themselves, nor suffer them that were entering to go in. I remember that when I was a child, we had a minister who would one Lord's day preach up holiness, and the next Lord's day preach against the practice of holiness.

II. And now, my brethren, I come in the next place to speak of the second part, 'Stand fast.' And because I see a hurricane a-coming, keep your ground, stand fast, and live in the Lord here, that you may live with him hereafter.

STAND FAST IN THE LORD

Therefore, my brethren dearly beloved and longed for, my joy and crown, so stand fast in the Lord, my dearly beloved.
Philippians 4:1

From this Scripture you have seen that the highest officers of the church of Christ, though they bear rule in the church, yet they are but brethren to the meanest saint. You have seen that it befits a true spiritual minister of Christ to have a most vehement, ardent, strong, melting, tender affection to that flock or people which the providence of God has committed to his charge. And you have seen that the fixed standing, flourishing, and thriving of that flock in the profession and practice of gospel-knowledge and obedience is matter of transcendent joy and triumph to such a godly pastor. That which I would now set forth is this: that it is the grand and indispensable duty of all sincere saints, in the most black and shaking seasons, to stand fast, fixed, and steadfast in the Lord.

This is a grand thing St Paul had to say to the Philippians when he was ready to have his head cut off; for so it was, he was beheaded for the testimony of Jesus. This is all he had to say when in gaol and in bonds, and that under heathen Romans: You are now my joy, you are now my crown. Oh! do but stand, and my joy will strike all the notes in the gamut of praise. Oh! do but stand, and my crown is studded with diamonds. We live if you stand, though we die when you stand.

It is the great and indispensable duty of all sincere saints, in the most black and shaking seasons, to stand fast, fixed and steadfast in the Lord. Whether these are black and shaking seasons, I have nothing to say, but I am speaking now entirely upon your duty, beloved; and for God's sake let the words of a civilly dying minister prevail with you. There is a kind of a maxim among some that, in case a person seemingly die and then revive again, the last words that were spoken by that person when in a rational condition are the only things which that person will remember when brought to life again. It is most probable, beloved, whatever others may think—it is my opinion (though God may work wonders)—that neither you nor I shall ever see the faces of or have a word to speak to one another till the day of judgment. Therefore I beseech you hear me as those that would and may live with me to eternity. Mark your duty; I have spoken something concerning the pastor's duty in my morning discourse; now for the people's, which is to stand fast, fixed and steadfast in the Lord. I confess I have a love for the whole auditory. I have a mess for them, but my Benjamin's mess[1] is for those I once called my own people. You are my Benjamins; I wish I had more than a fifth for you. This proposition I shall first prove, and then secondly improve.

In the worst of times, in the most shaking seasons (and if I am not greatly mistaken, there is an hour of temptation threatened by God, which now begins to be inflicted) if ever you would stand, stand now. For your comfort, let me but hint that a Christian may stand comfortably, when he falls sadly—that is, he may stand by God, when he falls by man. I knew that a great many years ago.

First, then, it is our duty to stand. There are Scriptures more than enough to prove this to be your duty. 'Stand perfect and complete in all the will of God' (*Col.* 4:12). 'Only let your conversation be as becometh the gospel of Christ; that whether I come and see you' (alas, poor Paul! you come and see them! you were beheaded before you could come and see them!), 'or else be absent, I may hear of your affairs, that ye stand fast in one spirit, with one mind striving together' (not to pluck out one another's throats, but striving together, not against one another) 'for the faith of the gospel' (*Phil.* 1:27). 'Therefore, my beloved brethren, be ye steadfast, unmoveable, always abounding in the work of the Lord, forasmuch as ye know that your labour is not in vain in the Lord' (*1 Cor.* 15:58). It is our duty to stand.

In what must we stand fast? I have no new doctrine to preach now. I shall but remind you of what I have

[1] See Genesis 43:34; Benjamin's portion of food from Joseph was five times that of any of his brothers.—P.

formerly spoken when you would not believe. I confess I do not begin to be of a new judgment now, and should I be allowed to continue in the ministry (a mercy I can hardly hope for) I should be of the same judgment and preach this same doctrine: Stand fast. God will certainly bring the people of God in England to his own terms, or else farewell to them forever. What is that we should be steadfast in? I would advise you to a steadfastness of judgment, of resolution, of faith, and of conscience. So stand fast in the Lord in your judgment, in your resolution, in your faith, and in your conscience.

I would advise you to be steadfast in *judgment*. Strange doctrines are the greatest fetters that assault a sound judgment; they are like waves which, if they do not split, will shake the ship to purpose. Therefore your duty is to cast anchor well, to stand firm on the rock of truth—I had almost said, in a word, all Protestant truth. Though the market may rise somewhat high, yet stand firmly there. While strange doctrines like so many impetuous waves are beating upon you, break themselves in pieces they may, but if you stand, they can never hurt you. I am not intending now to warn you against popery, although from the Scriptures I am apt to think the wound of the beast must be healed; however, do not you make a plaster for the beast to heal his wound. Be no more children tossed to and fro, carried about with every wind of doctrine, with every wind of windy doctrine, by the sleight of men and cunning craftiness that can cog the die.[1] Notable gamesters there are

[1] 'Cog the die' = Cheat by loading the dice—P.

in the world, but you must stand steady in judgment, you must be firm to your principles. I would have you stars, not meteors, for meteors are carried about with every blast of wind. I hope better things of you. I shall pray that God would make you steadfast in judgment. First, be sure to get good principles, and secondly, be sure to stand in those principles that you have got. And though I cannot say but some tares are to be found sown in this parish, yet I bless the Lord for the generality; I hope I may say I have an orthodox ministry.

It is not enough to stand in judgment, but we must be steadfast in our *resolution*. 'Be ye stedfast, unmoveable' (*1 Cor.* 15:58), such as stand firm on some basis and foundation that does not totter and stagger. If they find you staggering, to be sure the next moment they look upon you as falling. Be like the poles of the heavens; though all the world turns, the poles, they say, are immovable. If I am not mistaken, you may see a great turn in the world, and behold at this day the greatest turn that ever was in England; but yet you must not move, you must not stir. Be true to your resolutions, be just to your first love. Go on in the Lord's work; let nothing take you off. If I have preached any false doctrine among you, witness against me at the day of judgment; but if the things I have preached are true, stand to the truth. If you do not witness against my doctrine (mine it is not) rather witness for it. Remember that if you leave it, that very doctrine will witness against you at the day of judgment. Oh! that excellent heroine, queen Esther: 'Thus and thus will I do, and if I perish, I perish.' You cannot imagine against how many thousand temptations a steadfast resolution will guard you.

Then there is steadfastness in *faith*, when we so believe that we do not waver, or do not hesitate. Will you give me leave to propose to you, my dear friends (though my congregation I cannot call you), that question which our Saviour did unto the Jews: 'The baptism of John, whence was it? from heaven, or of men?' The doctrines you have heard, have they been from heaven, or from men? Answer me. If from men, abhor them, for man is a false creature, who would make merchandise of your faith and souls. But if from heaven, why then should you not believe them? I bless the Lord, my conscience bears me witness, I have never proposed a doctrine to you which I would have you believe, without Scripture warrant. If the doctrines have been from God, believe them. If not, abhor them, and any of those that shall dare to bring you doctrines but dare not bring the authority of the Scripture to warrant them. You must not be like those that waver 'like a wave of the sea driven with the wind and tossed' (*James* 1:6). The most godly man may stumble in his way and tread away, but a wavering-minded man is never settled concerning this way. Blessed be God, I am not now on this day (that looks as much like my dying day as it can be in the world) to begin to fix upon a religion or fix upon my way. I know my way, if God will but keep my steps and guide me in that way. If God be God (I appeal to your consciences) worship him. If Baal be God, worship him. Do not stand disputing and doubting. Do not say, shall I? shall I? If the ways you have found are the ways of God, follow them. God has but one way to heaven; there is but one truth. If Baal be God, follow Baal; do not stand wavering; do not consult with flesh and blood. It is an infinite mercy that God will give to any of us to leave relations, estates, congregations, anything for Christ. It is an infinite mercy we do not split upon a rock. Be sure to be either for God or Baal. A godly man many times halts in his way, but never halts between two opinions.

We also need steadfastness of *conscience*. Indeed the genius of my ministry has lain this way, and here I could easily launch out, but I must be short. I would speak a word in season to those that are weak: it becomes you to be steadfast in conscience. Hold fast to a God who decrees, to a Christ who redeems, to a Spirit who quickens, to a gospel which promises, to a heaven which is prepared, to a God who is infinitely more ready to save you than you can possibly be desirous to be saved by him. Be steadfast in conscience against the guilt, the filth of sin, and against the temptations of Satan. Let us draw near with full assurance of faith; you can never believe God's love so much as God's love engages you to believe.

Furthermore, you must be steadfast in *practice*. It is not the running well, but the reaching the goal; it is not the fighting, but the conquering that gives you title to the reward. For you to give a great deal of milk and kick it all over at length with your foot may argue you to have a good breast but a bad foot. Never give those beasts of Babylon occasion to say that a man may be a child of God in the morning and a child of the devil at night. Let us see to it that we never contradict our doctrine by our lives.

But why must we be steadfast? Alas, why? Would you have me marshal up all the reasons? Bid me count the stars or number the sands on the seashore. There is not an attribute in God, not a precept, promise, or threatening in the Word, not an ordinance, not a providence, there is nothing in God, or in the devil, or in sinners, or ourselves, but all would provide arguments to prove that saints should be steadfast. I must but hint at a few things.

First, I would argue from Jesus Christ. Believers, you love Christ, and therefore you love the honour of Christ; now the honour of Christ is highly engaged in our steadfastness. We never cast a deeper blot on the honour of Christ than when we cease to be steadfast. I need not tell you, for the Jesuits, those meek Papists, will tell you—those that delight in nothing more than in the milk of the Virgin Mary and in the blood of saints—they have enough if you are unsteady.

When you grow unsteady, you dishonour Christ in his sufferings. Pray tell me, believers, why did Christ sweat blood? Why did he die? Why did he undergo what the wrath of devils could inflict? Was it not for this end, to make you stand in that conquest triumphing? Remember Joshua's words: 'Come near, put your feet upon the necks of these kings' (*Josh.* 10:24). Christ died that you might live, that you might stand; and what dishonour to the eternal Saviour of the world, to a dying Saviour, to see a flying Christian! It was never heard of, that soldiers should fly before a conquered enemy whose legs were cut off, whose arms were broken, and whose swords were taken from them.

Lack of steadfastness is a dishonour to the Spirit of Christ, the same Spirit that was with Christ in all his agonies. This very Spirit he has given to believers, that he might bring them through with some victory. Therefore when we do not stand, it is a high dishonour to Christ's Spirit.

It is also a dishonour to Christ's truth. Oh! let but a saint fall, and what dishonour to Christ's truth! Oh! let but a saint fall, and what dishonour it brings to the truth. I have but thought of some recent experiences of poor ministers that I have heard of, who were carried about in triumph. Look, they said, here is the man that has done this, that, and the other thing! and now look, here he is!—I cannot excuse Noah for his drunkenness, yet methinks it is the part of a Ham to show his father's nakedness. I remember a person telling me (and a great truth it is!) that religion never suffers greater wounds than by the hands of her professed friends. Oh! what advantage have the wicked Papists taken against us in this land by the falls of professed Christians, both in principle and practice.

A fall from steadfastness is a very great dishonour to Christ's all-sufficiency. Tell me, man, is your Christ able to protect you against all evil? and is he able to supply you with all good, or is he not? If he is not, then deny him, and whatsoever you have said concerning him. If he is, then stand close to him: in the mount he will be seen.

Secondly, I would argue from the saints. Consider the infinite advantage that in the long run (I do not say immediately) will redound to those that are steady in judgment, in resolution, in faith, in conscience, in practice, so far as all these are conformable to the Word of God, and no further. The greatest advantage appears upon four grounds. Whatever you think, a steady condition is the safest condition, the fullest condition, the strongest condition, and the freest condition.

Oh! that I could beat this into my heart, as well as it is in my head. The safest condition in the midst of dangers, the fullest condition in the midst of wants, the strongest condition in the midst of assaults, the freest condition in the midst of straits! I profess in the presence of God, I have felt these things, and knew them to be true many years ago.

A steady condition is the *safest* condition. Never do the saints take hurt but by declining, by moving from their centre. While they remain at their centre the devil cannot touch them; departing thence is like the poor bird from her nest, everyone has a fling at them. Remember this, let but a man once leave his scriptural station, and what temptation is he able to stand against? It is just like a man thrown down from the top of a house, no stopping till he come to the bottom. 'He that is begotten of God keepeth himself, and that wicked one toucheth him not' (*1 John* 5:18).

A steady condition is the *fullest* condition. Oh! my

brethren, saints living steadfastly on their foundation are continually supplied by God, as the fountain continually pours itself into the streams. I know it is best living wholly upon God. How many thousands there are yet living in England who can tell you that they never enjoyed more of God, than when they enjoyed least of the creature. Some have professed to me that their prison was to them as a palace. They were troubled more with these things than ever you were, and the God of heaven grant you never may.

A steady condition is the *strongest* condition. A man that stands steadfast is like a man on a rock; as the waters come, they may dash themselves in pieces, but never shall be able to dash him in pieces. He is fixed on a rock and therefore stands. A man that stands steady to his scriptural principles is like Samson with his locks about him. Let all the Philistines come, what cares he? He is able to conquer them all.

A steady condition is the *freest* condition. A man that deserts his principles is a slave to every condition, afraid of every turn of events, of every aspen leaf in the world. He thinks all those are informers that converse with him. But he that stands fast by the power of the Spirit of God enjoys liberty and freedom. A man who is in chains as Paul was at Rome is in a far freer condition than others not troubled by that restraint. Well then, it is rational that you stand. But it may be that your lusts and interests can hardly swallow these things. If you stand you will not fall; if you do not stand, be sure you will fall at last.

The next thing I would do is to apply this truth. Is it the most important duty of all sincere professors of the faith, in the most shaking seasons, to stand steadfast in the Lord? Then let us make lamentations over our own souls and over hundreds of congregations. We say hundreds, nay thousands of congregations, that are this day, though they do not accompany us in person, yet are mingling their tears with ours and especially as I hear in the west of England.

Let us make a lamentation over our hearts. We must stand; this is our duty. Oh, how should it cause us to lie low, by reason of the instability of our hearts, and their declining from the true foundation every day! Alas, beloved, it is this that God complains of. 'They are a generation whose spirit is not steadfast with God' (*Psa.* 78:8), and therefore we have very much reason to complain of it. Oh, what an unsettled people have we been! One day we have been apt to cry, 'Hosanna, Hosanna, to the Son of David'; the next day our note is changed, 'Crucify him, crucify him, give us Barabbas.' Today the Lord is God, tomorrow Baal. Anything is God, provided we may keep our estates. Oh, Lord! what wilt thou do with such a people as this? Certainly it is a lamentation, and ought to be a lamentation. Believe it, beloved, I can now count seven years, if not something more, in which I have most clearly expected the days I now see. No way but the severest is to be taken with such a false people as we have been. Judge in your own thoughts whether we have been true to God or man, to saints or sinners, to the church of God at home or abroad; whether or no this be not matter of lamentation.

Let us make a lamentation with respect to our congregations. (It is not yet against the law to call them *our* congregations.) This, I confess, I can rather weep than speak about. I cannot speak, my heart is too big for my head here. Lord, is it the duty of people, of saints, to stand, to be steadfast? How then should we mourn over the poor souls who, because their pillars are taken away, must needs, for ought we know, fall unless thou dost support them? What, Lord, dost thou complain of a flock of sheep that are scattered? There is no wonder in it if their shepherd is gone. Do you look on it as a strange thing to see a poor ship tossed here and there in the sea, when her pilot is destroyed? Why, mother, is it a strange thing for your children to fall and knock their arms, legs, and even their brains out when their mother is taken from them? Oh, poor people! Good God, provide for this congregation! Aye, and for this city which (let defaming, abominable wretches say what they will) is certainly one of the best cities God has in the world; and therefore they hate it so desperately, because God loves it, and because they hate the God that loves it. I bless God that I can speak of my own people; they are not a mad pestiferous[1] people for the most of them. How many thousands have their hearts in their mouths now at this time before God in England! Alas, alas, that we should have our seers carried away from us; but what think you, when poor people shall be exposed to

[1] That is, 'troublesome' or 'annoying.'—P.

greater temptations, to an ulcer in the very kidneys, to a plague in the very heart or head? You now fear it, but when you feel it, what then?

By way of exhortation, beloved, I remember how good Jacob, when he was come into Egypt, ready to die, calls his children together and, before he dies, blesses his children. I cannot say you are my children, but I can say, in the strength of God, you are dearer to me than the children of my own bowels. I remember what poor Esau said, 'Hast thou but one blessing, my father? bless me, even me also, Oh, my father!' Oh, beloved! I have a few blessings for you; and for God's sake, take them as if they dropped from my lips when dying. It is very probable we shall never meet again until the day of judgment. Whatever others think, I am utterly against all irregular ways. I have (I bless the Lord) never had a hand in any change of government in all my life. I am for prayers, tears, quietness, submission, and meekness, and let God do his work; that will be best done when he does it. Therefore be exhorted to stand fast in the Lord. My own people, hear me now: though you should never hear me again, be exhorted to stand fast in the Lord. You are not a schismatical, heretical people. I do not know the least person among you inclining to popery: therefore, be exhorted, as you have been a people that have waited upon the ordinances of God, that have not persecuted your poor ministers, that have made it your design and business to live lovingly, quietly, and as it becomes Christians. I am confident a minister may live as comfortably among you as among any people in England. 'So be ye stedfast, unmoveable, always abounding in the work of the Lord, forasmuch as ye know that your labour is not in vain in the Lord.' Here I had prepared, I confess, several arguments to have moved you to this steadfastness.

I could have told you that if anyone of you turn back, you will meet with great temptations that will very much unfit you for heaven. 'If any man or woman draw back, my soul [saith God] shall have no pleasure in him.' I could have urged you with examples from the heathens. Alexander, being in India, bade them tell him the greatest rarity in their country. 'Sir, go tell them,' say they, 'when you return to Greece, there are many here that cannot be forced by the prowess of Alexander to change their minds.' I know there are some here that cannot be easily persuaded to change their religion. Lactantius says, 'Our very women torment their tormentors.' I would never desire a more able disputant than a woman against a monk.

I could tell you of those enjoyments God has given you. Our miseries have been great, but our mercies have been greater. I could tell you of six troubles and of seven; of six in which God has stood by, and of seven in which he has not forsaken; and the truth is, he cannot forsake his people. He may forsake them as to comfort, but he will never forsake them as to support. Let him lay on a burden, he will be sure to strengthen the back.

I hope it is not dangerous if I tell you that you are engaged to God. There are vows upon you, baptismal vows, to say no more. You have sworn to God, you have lifted up your hands; you are those that have undertaken that you would be true to God to your lives' end. Oh, remember Zedekiah's case:

> Seeing he despised the oath by breaking the covenant, when, lo, he had given his hand, and hath done all these things, he shall not escape. Therefore thus saith the Lord GOD; As I live, surely mine oath that he hath despised, and my covenant that he hath broken, even it will I recompense upon his own head' (Ezek. 17:18, 19).

Remember this: you may play fast and loose with man, but you must not think ever to carry it off by playing fast and loose with God.

If you should not stand, you lose all you have wrought. All your prayers, tears, professions, practices, sufferings, are all gone if you give in at last.

While you stand by God, God has promised to stand by you; and the truth is, I have but one God, what matters all the titles possessed by worms? Should there be a thousand devils, yet all those devils are in one chain, and the end of that chain is in the hand of one God. Oh! God will show himself strong, 'For the eyes of the LORD run to and fro throughout the whole earth, to shew himself strong in the behalf of them whose heart is perfect toward him' (2 *Chron.* 16:9).

You may say, what shall I do in order to stand?

I answer: If ever you would stand, if ever you would be firm standing Christians indeed, make certain you are not light and proud Christians. A feather will never stand against a whirlwind. Error and profaneness are most apt to breed in proud hearts. The proud and blasphemers are put together (2 *Tim.* 3:2). Be but humble Christians—that is the way to be standing steady Christians. If ever you would be steady in your stations you must be low in your own eyes.

Soon we shall have another kind of religion come up, as we have had it a great while. So-and-so cannot be an honest man; alas, he is a Presbyterian, he is an Independent, he is an Anabaptist! and in these present days, we shall often hear it said, so-and-so cannot be a good and honest man, for he does not conform: or, on the other hand, he cannot be an honest man, for he does conform. These are poor things. I bless God, I lay not the stress of my salvation upon these. It is true, I cannot in conscience conform, but I do not lay the stress of salvation on it, as I did not lay the stress of my salvation on my being a Presbyterian. I confess I am so, and have been; it has been my unhappiness to be always on the sinking side, yet I lay not the stress of my salvation upon it. It is my conscience, but it may be I have not so much light as another man; and I profess, in the presence of God, could I conform without sin to my own conscience, I would. If I were to do anything against my conscience, I should sin and break my peace and conscience and all, and never see a good day.

Do not then spend the strength of your zeal for your religion in censuring others. The man that is most busy in censuring others is always least employed in examining himself. Remember good John Bradford, who would not censure Bonner nor Gardiner, though, said he, 'They call John Bradford the hypocritical John Bradford.'

Look you to the main things, look into your own hearts, examine them, and then you will not be much occupied in censuring others.

You must beware of being loose Christians. Will you remember one thing from me? (the God of heaven grant that you may never live to see it verified)—a loose Protestant is one of the fittest persons in the world to make a strict Papist. Tell me not of the Protestantism of a drunkard; it is because his king and country are Protestants where he lives. There is no religion in one who lives loosely. If ungodliness is in the heart, it is no difficult thing for error to get into the head. A loose heart can best comply with loose principles and take up with any religion in the world that is uppermost. If the Turks prevail, the man of loose heart will soon be of their religion.

Again, take heed of being worldly Christians. Oh! this is the David that has slain his ten thousands. A worldly heart will be bought and sold upon every turn to serve the devil's turn. Come to one of a worldly heart, promise him thirty pieces of silver, and he will betray his Saviour. The temptations of the world are great upon us at this time. You that are husbands and parents know it. The world is a great temptation, but if we are overcome by the world, and the world is not overcome by us, we shall never be able to overcome any one temptation that is offered to us. Therefore that is an admirable support, 'In the world ye shall have tribulation: but be of good cheer, I have overcome the world.' I have overcome the world for you; and likewise I have overcome the world in you. Oh, Lord! if thou wilt but overcome the love and fear of the world, if thou wilt but arm us against the smiles of the world, then come what will, we shall stand steadfast.

Take heed also of being hypocritical Christians. Take heed you do not receive the truth without receiving the truth in the love of that truth. You have received the truth, but have you received the truth in the love of that truth which you have received? Want of this gives damnable occasion to popery; 'and with all deceivableness of unrighteousness in them that perish; because they received not the love of the truth, that they might be saved' (2 *Thess.* 2:10). It is just with God that they should fall into errors whose hearts did never love real truths. Better never to have received the truth, than to receive it, and not in the love of it.

Take heed of being venturous and God-tempting Christians. What is that? When do I tempt God? I tempt God when I run into a pest-house and say God will preserve me from the plague. Take heed of running into temptations to sin, whether in principles or in practice. I could tell you of two spiritual pest-houses in England, if I had time; one in its principles, and one in its practice. I do not say that I mean playhouses on the one hand or mass-houses on the other. Certainly, brethren, I read of Julian, that wicked apostate, that he sank into his apostacy first by going to hear Libanius preach. Do not mistake me; I am not against your going to hear the ministers of Christ, for a man may be a true minister, though he be a bad man. All the world can never answer the case of Judas, who was a true minister, though a bad man. While I plead for the truth of his ministry, I do not spread a skirt over the wickedness of his life. The scribes and Pharisees sit in Moses' chair; hear them.

But that which I mainly aim at is this. Do not go and run and venture yourself into temptations. You have heard of a superstitious or idolatrous worship; you are curious to see this. What if, when you are found in Satan's way, Satan should lay his paw on you and claim you? What do you there in Satan's ground? Would you be found, when you come to die, in a playhouse? or in a place where the true God is idolatrously worshipped? It is a great truth—if you would not be found in the devil's power, do not be found in the devil's pound. Brethren, we must know Satan is busy enough to tempt us; we need not go to tempt him. Eve lost all she had by hearing one sermon, but it was from the devil. Therefore, if you would not have your pockets picked, do not trade amongst cheaters. 'If any man teach otherwise [than what ye have received, and we have preached] . . . from such withdraw thyself' (*1 Tim.* 6:3, 5). That is, a good, honest, laudable separation; from such withdraw thyself.

Where God does not find a mouth to speak, you must not find an ear to hear, nor a heart to believe. This is one of the grand points in my chart and compass on which I hope I shall venture all. If any man come with a doctrine not according to the Word of God, let him carry it whither he will, what have I to do with it? Either he comes from God or no. If he shows me God's Word, then I will believe; if not, go your way, open your pack where else you please. Where God does not find a mouth to speak; where there is not a precept, promise, threatening, or example in the Word of God; let them talk their hearts out; it is nothing to me, to my religion, to my salvation.

You may object and say: But what ground have you for this? I answer: Jesuit, I will tell you my ground: this is my great argument against popery. Could men convince me that I must believe with an implicit faith because they say it, I think it would not be long before I turned Papist. You say again: But why must I not believe it with an implicit faith? I answer: Look at three great Scriptures, first, Matthew 15:2: 'Why do thy disciples transgress the tradition of the elders?' The Jews come and tell Christ that he was not a true son of the church of the Jews. He was disobedient to the church of the Jews. Why? Because they say, Thou hast disciples that walk not as they ought. What do they do? They commit an unpardonable sin, they transgress the tradition of the elders, they break one of the greatest commandments. What is that tradition? They wash not their hands when they eat bread: this was the great sin, eating with unwashed hands, and they charge it on him. Why do you bring in this tradition? What have you to say for it? What is that to the purpose? Prove, O Jesus of Nazareth, that there is anything in the Word of God that is against washing? But, says he, prove you out of the Word of God where they are bound to wash before they eat. If you will impose this as a rule, show your authority for it. And let me tell you, you that talk of tradition, first you set up an altar God never thought of; and secondly, you pull down God's altar. Why do you all transgress the commandments of God by your tradition?

> God commanded, saying, Honour thy father and mother: and, He that curseth father or mother, let him die the death. But ye say, Whosoever shall say to his father or his mother, It is a gift, by whatsoever thou mightest be profited by me; And honour not his father or his mother, he shall be free. Thus have ye made the commandment of God of none effect by your tradition. Ye hypocrites, well did Esaias prophesy of you, saying, This people draweth nigh unto me with their mouth, and honoureth me with their lips; but their heart is far from me (*Matt.* 15:4-8).

They draw near, wash their hands, wash their cups, and have filthy souls; they honour me with their lips only. But men may say, though their principle, their heart, is bad, their worship is good. But no, 'in vain they do worship me, teaching for doctrines the commandments of men.'

So then, my brethren, remember that all those that teach for doctrines the precepts of men, worship God in vain. Here is an innocent command, you must wash before you eat; if you do not wash, you transgress the tradition of the elders. Yet if you starve father and mother, and but give to the church, to a nunnery, to a friary, it is all one. So that all those that will for doctrines teach the traditions of men, and that render the commandments of God of none effect, 'In vain do they worship me,' says the Lord. Therefore wherever God does not find a tongue to speak, you must not find an ear to hear, not an heart to believe. Christians, if you expect Christ's benediction, always call aloud for Christ's word of institution.

Another Scripture is Colossians 2:18 which is one of the greatest texts you have against popery: 'Let no man beguile you of your reward in a voluntary humility and worshipping of angels, intruding into those things which he hath not seen, vainly puffed up by his fleshly mind.' Another is Deuteronomy 12:32: 'What thing soever I command you, observe to do it: thou shalt not add thereto, nor diminish from it.' There are no wens[1] in the body of God's precepts, therefore none of them are to be cut off. You must not deal with God's ordinances, as that tyrant Procrustes did with men; if they were too long for his bed, he would cut them shorter; if too short, he would pull their limbs out of joint to make them longer. Never think yourselves bound in conscience to lend an ear to that which God does not find a mouth to speak.

Would you stand fast? Then beware of shaking doctrines. What are those? There are a great many such doctrines. Give me leave to instance three or four.

As you love your souls, beware of doctrines that tend to and preach up licentiousness, looseness, and profaneness. Should any tell you that you may lawfully violate and profane the sabbath, do not believe it. The doctrine of

[1] That is, 'warts' or 'cysts'.—P.

the gospel is a doctrine of godliness: it teaches us to deny ungodliness and wordly lusts and to live soberly, righteously, and godly in this present world. Therefore if you find any doctrine at any time that shows the least tendency to encourage you in any sin, know that it is a doctrine against the gospel.

Wherever you find any doctrine that tends to the lifting up of a man's free will and the debasing of God's free grace, know that it is a wicked doctrine and against the genius of the gospel. Perhaps the Papists will tell you that you are alive, but Paul tells us we are dead. They say that we can do anything. They say that we can save ourselves and close with Christ if we will, whereas the apostle tells us, 'The natural man receiveth not the things of the Spirit of God: for they are foolishness unto him: neither can he know them, because they are spiritually discerned' (*1 Cor.* 2:14). It may be they will tell you that a natural man may love God with his heart really and savingly, whereas the apostle tells you, 'The carnal mind is enmity against God: for it is not subject to the law of God, neither indeed can be' (*Rom.* 8:7). Remember that in all those doctrines in which we agree with those whom we call Pelagians and Arminians, so far we agree with the Jesuits and the worst of Papists.

As you would avoid hell, avoid all those doctrines that would lift up self-righteousness and debase the righteousness of Christ. I confess I am against forty things in popery, but my whole soul is here engaged in what I say, for if their doctrine is true, I never expect salvation by God. Either I must be saved by Christ alone or else I must not be saved by Christ at all. Though Christ will never save me without sanctification, yet Christ never intended that my sanctification should merit his salvation. Be as holy as you can, as if there were no gospel to save you. Yet when you are as holy as you can, you must believe in Christ as if there were no law at all to condemn you. Tell me of the merit of saints: I will believe it, when I believe the whore of Babylon to be Christ's spouse.

Would you stand fast? Then you must be praying Christians. I confess when most of my strings are broken, there is yet one that holds; there is a spirit of prayer among the saints of God. I can pray yet; and I had rather stand against the canons of the wicked than against the prayers of the righteous. Oh! pray that you enter not into temptation; or, if we enter into temptation, Lord, let not the temptation enter into us! Pray, if possible, let this cup pass from me, but if not, let it not poison me, but let me be bettered by it, and in due time deliver me from it. I believe it would be a great temptation to you, if it should be said to you, 'You shall trade with no man any more; you have enjoyed such and such comforts, now bid them adieu for ever, you shall have no more to do with them.' This would be a temptation. Temptations and trials are great, and certainly where they are so, prayer should be strong. There is no relief to be expected from earth; all our relief is to be expected from God and that is to be obtained by prayer. Pray that God would be pleased above all things in the world to make you sincere. If you would be steadfast in your profession, you must be sincere in your practice. 'To him that hath shall be given,' that is a comfort; to him that hath but truth of grace, to him shall be given growth of grace. Would you be steady Christians? Then make it your great work to attend the ordinances, which God has prescribed to make you steady Christians. You were told of this many years ago, concerning attending the ordinances of God.

It may be you cannot be so much in the pulpit as you would like. Oh! be more in secret prayer. It may be you will not have so many opportunities to hear so many lectures; be more conscientious in your meditations in secret. It may be you will not have that freedom with God in public; be more earnest with God in private.

Mind your families more than ever. You have your children and servants who call aloud upon you. How many grave faces do I see at this time, that can tell me, Sir, I remember some twenty or thirty years ago, you could not pass along the streets but in various houses there was one family repeating the Word of God, another singing the praises of God, another praying to God, another conferring concerning the things of God. At that time we had not so many foolish absurd excursions into streets and fields as now. Oh! for the Lord's sake, begin to take up these family duties now. Let the Amorite, Perizzite, and Jebusite do what they will; but as for you and your children and your servants, serve the Lord. Up again with those godly exercises! When you cannot hear a sermon, then read a sermon. If we could hear a sermon well preached, our godly parents would engage us to read a sermon well penned. If there is nothing new, let the Word repeated and meditated call to mind what you have heard. Oh! reduce yourselves to your Christian frame. Let the debauched atheists know that they have something among you to be feared, that is, your prayers. Let them know that though you have not those opportunities that you once had, yet you will improve those you have. And you, masters of this parish, for God's sake, keep in your servants on this day more than ever. You are accountable for their souls; and they will give you a thousand thanks when they come to age, especially at the day of judgment. They will then say, Blessed be God I had such a master! Blessed be God I had such a mistress! Blessed be God I had such parents!

But you will say, what would you have us do for public ordinances? I answer: Wherever Christ finds a tongue to speak, I am bound to find an ear to hear and a heart to believe. I would not be mistaken. I bless the Lord I am not turned out of my ministry for being a schismatic (I know schism is a sin) nor know I any of my brethren that are so. Do not mistake us, therefore; do not go and tell the Jesuits we are schismatics, for it is not so. But this I would advise (I speak as though I were dying) do whatever lies in your power to hear such whom you think to be godly. Beg of God, be earnest with him, that he would give pastors after his own heart. Not such as daub with untempered mortar, not such as prophesy lies in the name of the Lord, not such as are clouds without water, but such as are guides of the blind, burning and shining lights, faithful stewards. What must you do?

What did you do twenty or thirty years ago? What did the good old Puritans do? They were not schismatics. But, as much as lies in you, hear them whom in your consciences you judge God hears. Oh! then expect the Word of God should come to your hearts, when you have ground to believe it comes from your pastor's heart. I must confess, I intend to do the same, when put into the same condition with you. I acknowledge I am bound in conscience to hear the Word of God, but must take care whom I hear; I must hear those by whom God speaks. I hope God will grant several such.

Take this advice also, and then I have no more to say. Whatever abuse you find either in pastor, in people, or wherever you find it, do not begin as your old custom has been, to rail, calumniate, backbite, and speak behind their backs. This is wicked and ungodly. But let every one of us who are members of any visible church act according as God prescribes for us. What is that? If I know anything against my brother, do not go and make a sputter and a noise and backbite; but take the rule of Christ:

> If thy brother shall trespass against thee, go and tell him his fault between thee and him alone: if he shall hear thee, thou hast gained thy brother. But if he will not hear thee, then take with thee one or two more . . . and if he neglect to hear them, tell it unto the church (*Matt.* 18:15-17);

and leave the blood at their door. You have freed your own soul. I hope by God's grace I shall do so.

Thus I have now spoken something from this Scripture. I cannot speak what I desire; for besides the exhausting of my spirits, there is something to be done after, *viz.*, a funeral sermon. I shall say no more, but only this: the God of heaven be pleased to make you mind these plain things. I can truly say this: I have not spoken one word that I remember that I would not have said to you if I had been a-dying and called to go to God as soon as I had gone out of the pulpit. The God of peace be with you. Only mind that one thing—when God does not find a tongue to speak, do not find an ear to hear, nor a heart to believe.

THOMAS WATSON

LIFE

The origins of Thomas Watson, one of the most popular preachers of his time, are obscure, but, like many of his fellow-Puritans, he was educated at Emmanuel College, Cambridge, obtaining his B.A. in 1639 and his M.A. three years later. After preaching at Hereford in 1641, he settled at St Stephen's Church, Walbrook, in the following year and remained there until the Ejection. Watson's ministry seems to have been highly valued by his parishioners, as evidenced by increases in his salary over the years. Favouring ecclesiastical reform, he upheld the Westminster Confession, but remonstrated against the execution of Charles I, and in 1651 was involved in Love's plot to restore the Stuarts, as a result of which he was imprisoned for some months.

After 1662, Watson continued to preach privately in London and was more than once reported to the authorities as a conventicler. He was licensed to preach at his own house under the 1672 Declaration of Indulgence and was pastor of a congregation at Crosby Square, where Stephen Charnock joined him as co-pastor. When ill-health finally curtailed his ministry, he retired to

Barnston, Essex, and, dying in 1686, was buried there. Watson's printed works make it plain why he enjoyed such success as a preacher. His best-known work *A Body of Practical Divinity* has been reprinted many times, including the three-volume edition by The Banner of Truth Trust. These sermons, preached on the Shorter Catechism of the Westminster Assembly, are lively, full of pithy sayings, and eminently readable.

PRAYER

[*Thomas Watson's Prayer, at Walbrook, 8th July 1662*]

Oh, Lord God, all our springs are in thee. It is good for us to draw nigh to thee through Jesus Christ. Thou art all fulness, the quintessence of all sweetness, the centre of all blessedness. Thou art the Father of our Lord Jesus Christ, and in him our Father. Thou art our light. Thou givest us the blessed opportunities of enjoying communion with thyself, God blessed for ever.

These mercies are forfeited mercies; we have abused the blessings of thy house; we have grieved thy blessed Spirit. Therefore it is just for thee to deprive us of these comforts and to make us know the worth of these mercies by the want of them.

Lord, we desire to judge ourselves, that we may not be condemned with the world. Righteous art thou, Oh, Lord, and just in all thy judgments. We confess we are unworthy to have any converse with so holy a God; we are polluted dust and ashes, not worthy to tread thy courts; and it is of thy mercy that we are not consumed. How often have we plucked fruit from the forbidden tree! We have sinned presumptuously against the clearest light and the dearest love; always have we sinned. Thy footsteps have dropped fatness. Thou hast shown mercy to us, but the better thou hast been to us, the worse we have been to thee. Thou hast loaded us with thy mercies, and we have wearied thee with our sins. When we look into ourselves, oh, the poison of our natures! Whatever a leper touched, was unclean; thus by our spiritual leprosy we infect our holy things. Our prayers need pardon, and our tears need the blood of sprinkling to wash them. How vain are our vows! How sensual are our affections! We confess we are untuned and unstrung for every holy action; we are never out of tune to sin but always out of tune to pray. We give the world our main affections and our strong desires; whereas we should use this world as if we used it not. And alas, we pray as if we prayed not and serve thee as if we served thee not. There is not that reverence, nor that devotion, nor that activeness of faith that there should be.

Lord, if thou shouldst say thou wouldst pardon all our sins to this time and only judge us for this prayer, woe unto us! What breathings of unbelief and hypocrisy are there now, when we approach unto thee? We pray thee pardon us for Christ's sake. Who can tell how oft he offends? We can as well reckon the drops of the ocean as number our sins. We have filled up the number of the nation's sins, but we have not filled thy bottle with our tears. And that which exceedingly aggravates our sins is that we cannot mourn for sin; we can grieve for our losses but we cannot mourn for our unkindnesses. We have crucified the Lord of life. Sin has not only defiled us, but hardened us; nothing can melt us but the love of Christ, nothing can soften us but the blood of Christ. Oh, withhold not thy mercies from us. Oh, help us to eat the passover with bitter herbs. Let us look on Christ and weep over him. Let us look on a broken Christ with broken hearts and on a bleeding Christ with bleeding hearts. Let us mourn that we grieve the God who is always doing us good. Oh, humble us for our unkindness, and for Christ's sake blot out our transgressions; they are more than we can number, but not more than God can pardon.

Though we have lost the dutifulness of children, thou hast not lost the goodness of a father. Let us be held forth as patterns of mercy; so shall we trumpet forth thy praise to all eternity. Whatever afflictions thou layest upon our bodies, let not our sins be unpardoned; let not sin and affliction be together upon us. Let there be peace in heaven, and peace in the court of conscience. We have found this part of thy Word true, 'In the world we shall have trouble'; let us find the other part true, 'In Jesus Christ we shall have peace.' Oh, let peace and holiness go together. Make us new creatures, that we may be glorious creatures. Without faith Christ will not profit us. When we can call nothing in the world ours, let us call Christ ours. Lord, draw thine image every day more lively upon us; give us a more lively hope and a more inflamed love to Christ. Let us have a spirit of courage and resolution. Keep us from the fallacies of our own hearts. Keep us from the defilements of the times. Make us pure in heart that we may see God, that we may have gospel spirits, humble spirits, meek spirits. As Christ did take our flesh, let us partake of his Spirit. Why dost thou embitter the breast of the creature to us but that we should find the sweetness of the promises? There is as much in the promises as ever. Let us live upon God; let us cast anchor in heaven, and we shall never sink.

Shower down thy blessings (even the choicest of them) upon the head and heart of our dread Sovereign, Charles, by thy appointment of England, Scotland, France and Ireland, King, Defender of the faith. Let him see wherein his chiefest interest lies. Let him count those his best subjects that are Christ's subjects. Bless him in his royal consort, in his royal relations. Let the Lords of his Privy Council be a terror to evildoers and encouragers of those that do well.

Bless all thine ordinances to us; make them to be fulness of life to everyone before thee. We are come this day to partake of them; oh, pour in wine and oil into our souls. Let us be a watered garden. Let this blessed sacrament be a poison to our lust and nourishment for our grace. Hear us, be our God, follow us with mercy, crown us with acceptance, and all for Christ's sake, whom not seeing we love, in whom believing we rejoice. To Christ, with thee and the Holy Spirit, be glory, honour, and praise, now and forever, Amen.

WEAL TO THE RIGHTEOUS, BUT WOE TO THE WICKED

Say ye to the righteous, that it shall be well with him: for they shall eat the fruit of their doings. Woe unto the wicked! it shall be ill with him: for the reward of his hands shall be given him.
Isaiah 3:10, 11

This text is like Israel's pillar of cloud; it has a light side and a dark side. It has a light side unto the godly, 'Say unto the righteous, it shall be well with him'; and it has a dark side unto the wicked, 'Woe unto the wicked! it shall be ill with him.' Both, you see, are rewarded, righteous and wicked; but here is a vast difference: the one has a reward of mercy, the other a reward of justice.

I begin with the first of these: 'Say unto the righteous, it shall be well with him.'

This scripture was written in a very sad and calamitous time, as you may read in the beginning of the chapter. 'The mighty man, and the man of war, the judge, and the prophet, and the prudent, and the ancient' shall be taken away. This was a very sad time with the church of God in Jerusalem. If the judge be taken away, where will equity be found? If the prophet be removed, where will be any word from God? The whole body politic was running to ruin and falling into corruption. Now in this sad juncture, God would have this text to be written, and it is like a rainbow in the clouds. God would have his people comforted in the midst of afflictions. 'Say unto the righteous, it shall be well with them.'

The great proposition that lies in the words is this: However things may go in the world, it shall be well with the righteous man. This is an oracle from God's own mouth, and therefore we are not to dispute it. It is God's own oracle, 'Say unto the righteous, it shall be well with him.' I might multiply scriptures, but I will give you one instance from Ecclesiastes 8:12: 'Surely I know it shall be well with them that fear God.' I *know* it; it is a golden maxim not to be disputed; 'It shall be well with them that fear God.'

For the unfolding of this, the first thing to consider is, who is meant here by the righteous man? Now there is a threefold righteousness. First, a *legal* righteousness. In this sense Adam was said to be righteous, when he wore the robe of innocency. Adam's heart agreed with the law of God exactly, as a well-made dial goes with the sun; but this righteousness has been forfeited and lost.

Again, there is a *moral* righteousness. Thus, he is said to be righteous, who is adorned with the moral virtues, who is prudent and just and temperate, and who lives up to the common standard of morality.

Then there is an *evangelical* righteousness, and it is this that is meant here. This evangelical righteousness is twofold. It is a righteousness of imputation, and that is when Christ's righteousness is made over to us: and, beloved, this righteousness is as truly ours to justify us as it is Christ's to bestow it upon us. Again, it is a righteousness of implantation, which is nothing else but the infusing of the seed and habit of grace into the heart. It is planting of holiness in a man and making him a partaker of the divine nature. This is to be righteous in the sight of God—a righteousness of imputation and a righteousness of implantation.

The second thing to show you is why it shall go well with the righteous man, however things may go in the world. One reason is because he who is righteous has his greatest evils removed, his sin pardoned, and then it must needs be well with him. Sin is the thorn in a man's conscience; now when the thorn is plucked out by forgiveness and remission, then it is well with that man. Forgiveness in Scripture is called a lifting off of sin, 'Lord, why dost thou not lift off my sin?' (*Job* 7:21). So the Hebrew word signifies. It is a metaphor taken from the case of a weary man who goes under a burden. He is ready to sink under it, but another man comes and lifts off this burden; even so does the great God, when the burden of sin is ready to sink the conscience, God lifts off the burden of sin from the conscience, and lays it on Christ's shoulder, and he carries it. Now he that has this burden thus carried, it is well with him however things go.

Forgiveness of sin and pardon is a crowning blessing; it is the jewel of a believer's crown. Pardon of sin is a multiplying mercy, it brings a great many mercies along with it. Whom God pardons, he adopts; whom God pardons, he invests with grace and glory. So that this is a multiplying mercy; it is such a mercy that it is enough to make a sick man well. 'The inhabitant shall not say, I am sick: the people that dwell therein shall be forgiven their iniquity' (*Isa.* 33:24). The sense of pardon takes away the sense of pain, and then it must needs be well with the righteous, for his greatest evil is removed.

However things go, it is well with the righteous because God is his portion. 'The LORD is the portion of mine inheritance . . . The lines are fallen unto me in pleasant places' (*Psa.* 16:5, 6). In God all good things are found, and all that is in God is engaged for the good of the righteous. His power is there to help, his wisdom to teach, his Spirit to sanctify, and his mercy to save. God is the righteous man's portion, and can God give a greater gift to us than himself? God is a rich portion; he is the riches of the angels. God is a safe and sure portion, for his name is a strong tower. He is a portion that can never be spent, for he is the infinite one. He is a portion that can never be lost, for he is the eternal one. 'God is . . . my portion for ever' (*Psa.* 73:26). Surely it is well with the righteous man who has God for his portion. Is it not well with that man who is happy? Why, if God be our portion we are happy. 'Happy is that people . . . whose God is the LORD' (*Psa.* 144:15).

Here is abundance of comfort for every godly man, for

every person serving God in this congregation; God has sent me this day with a commission to comfort you. Oh! that I might drop the oil of gladness into every broken heart and make every troubled spirit rejoice. Oh, here is good news from heaven! 'Say unto the righteous, it shall be well with him.'

But there is a question that must be answered. You will say to me, How does it appear that it shall be well with the righteous? For we often see that he fares ill in this world; many times he is deprived of his comfort; he may lose his very life for the gospel's sake, and he is made the very reproach of the world. How then is it well with the righteous? To this I answer, that still it is well with the righteous, even though he meet with trouble in the world, and one trouble follows on the neck of another. Yet it is well with the righteous, as will appear in these three particulars:

1. The troubles that the righteous man meets with turn to good, and so it is well with him. That is a most famous scripture in Jeremiah 24:5: 'Whom I have sent out of this place into the land of the Chaldeans for their good.' God's own Israel were transported into Babylon among their enemies; but it is 'for their good, saith the LORD.' The troubles of the righteous are a means to purge out their sin. I have read a story of one who ran upon another with a sword to kill him; by accident his sword ran into an abscess, causing it to break. Thus all the evils and troubles of the righteous serve but to cure them of the abscess of pride, to make them more humble. When the body of a saint is afflicted, his soul

revives and flourishes in grace. At Rome there were two laurel trees, and when one withered the other flourished; so when the body is afflicted, the soul, the other laurel, revives and flourishes. Out of the bitterest drink God distils his glory and our salvation. Jerome says that what the world looks on as a punishment, God makes a medicine to heal the sore. So then, it shall be well with the righteous. The rod of God upon a saint is only God's pencil, by which he draws his image in more lively fashion on the soul. God never strikes the strings of his viol but to make the music sweeter. Thus it is well with the righteous.

2. In the midst of all the trouble that befalls the righteous, still it is well with them in regard of those inward heart-revivings that God gives them. We see a godly man's misery, but we do not see his comfort. We see his prison gates, but we do not hear the music that is within his conscience. God sweetens to his people outward trouble with inward peace. One title that is given to God is 'God, that comforteth those that are cast down' (2 *Cor.* 7:6). The bee can gather honey as well from the thistle and from the bitter herb as from the sweet flower; the child of God can gather joy out of sorrow: out of the very carcass sometimes the Lord gives honey. When the body is in pain, the soul may be at ease, as when a man's head aches, yet his heart may be well. Thus it is well with the righteous. God gives him that inward comfort that revives his soul and sweetens his outward pain.

3. In the time of trouble and calamity, still it is well with the righteous because God covers his people in

the time of trouble, he hides them in the storm. God has a care to hide his jewels and will not let them be carried away; and thus he makes good that scripture literally, 'he shall cover thee with his feathers, and under his wings shalt thou trust' (*Psa.* 91:4). God oftentimes verifies this scripture literally. He makes his angels to be his people's lifeguard, to hide them, and defend them. When a flood was coming upon the world, God provided an ark to hide Noah. When Israel is carried and transported to Babylon, God hid Jeremiah and gave him his life for a prey (*Jer.* 39:17, 18). It is in this sense that the saints of God are called his hidden ones (*Psa.* 83:3). Why so? Not only because they are hid in God's decree and hid in Christ's wounds, but oftentimes God hides them in a time of danger and calamity. He reserved to himself seven thousand that had not bowed the knee to Baal. The prophet knew not where there was one, but God knew there were seven thousand. In this sense, it is well with the righteous in time of public misery.

Aye, but you will say, Sometimes it goes worse with the righteous than all this. Sometimes they die and perish, they are carried away by a tempest. Why? Even so; yet still it is well with the righteous. Consider this: many times God takes away the righteous by death, and that in great mercy; he takes them away that they may not see the misery that comes upon a nation. Virgil, the heathen poet, says, 'They are happy that die before their country.' His meaning is that they die before they see the ruin of their country; and truly God many times takes away his people in mercy, that they may not see the ruin that is coming on a land. You will find an example of this in 1 Kings 14:13: 'He only of Jeroboam shall come to the grave [in peace], because in him there is found some good thing toward the LORD God of Israel.' God in mercy puts him in his grave early, so that he should not see the evil coming upon the land. There is a parallel to this in 2 Kings 22:20. It is spoken of Josiah: 'I will gather thee unto thy fathers, and thou shalt be gathered unto thy grave in peace; and thine eyes shall not see all the evil which I will bring upon this place.' Josiah died in battle: how then was it said he went to the grave in peace? We must understand the meaning of it to be this: Josiah went to his grave in peace because he was a holy man, and he had made his peace with God, and so he went to his grave in peace. In order that he should not see the evil approaching, God gathered him to his grave in peace.

Jerome speaking of his friend Nepotian (and Jerome lived to see some troubles before he died!) said, 'Oh! how happy is my friend Nepotian, that sees not these troubles, but is got out of the storm, and is arrived safe in heaven.' In mercy Luther died before the trouble in Germany broke forth: and thus you see, though the righteous die, yet it is well with them. God takes them away in mercy that they may not see approaching evils.

Though the righteous die and are taken away, yet it is well with them, because death cannot hurt them. Death can neither hurt their body nor yet their souls, and so it is well with them. The body of a saint does not perish, though it die; the bodies of the saints are very precious dust in God's account: precious dust! The Lord locks up these jewels in the grave as in a cabinet. The bodies of the saints lie mellowing and ripening in the grave till the blessed time of the resurrection. Oh! how precious is the dust of a believer! Though the world mind it not, yet it is precious unto God. The husbandman has some corn in his barn, and he has other corn in the ground: and the corn that is in the ground is as precious to him as that which is in the barn. The bodies of the saints shall be more glorious and blessed at the resurrection than ever they were before. Tertullian calls them angelical bodies because of the beauty and lustre that shall be upon them. As it is with your silks, when they are dyed a purple or scarlet colour, they are made more bright and illustrious than they were before; thus it is with the bodies of the saints—they shall be dyed of a better colour at the resurrection; they shall be made like Christ's glorious body (*Phil.* 3:21). Thus it shall be well with the righteous, for their bodies shall not perish.

It will be well with the righteous at death with regard to their souls too. Oh, it will be a blessed time! Methinks it is with a saint at the time of death just as it was with Saint Paul in his voyage to Rome. We read that the ship did break up, but though there were so many broken pieces, yet he got safe to shore; so though the ship of the believer's body break by death, yet it is safe with the passenger; his soul gets safe to the heavenly harbour. Let me tell you, the day of a believer's death is the birthday of his blessedness; it is his ascension-day to heaven. The day of his death is his marriage-day with Jesus Christ.

Faith does but contract us here. In this life is only the betrothal, but at death the nuptials shall be solemnized in glory. The righteous shall see God face to face. It will be heaven enough to have a sight of God, says Augustine, when the saints shall enter into joy. Here joy enters into them, but there they shall enter into joy. They shall drink of those pure rivers that run from the everlasting fountain.

And thus you see that it will be well with the righteous, however things go. Though trouble come, though death come, yet it will go well with the righteous. And so let those that are the people of God comfort themselves in these words! Oh, what an encouragement is this to all you that hear me to begin to be righteous! This text may tempt us all to be godly. 'Say unto the righteous, it shall be well with him.' When things are never so ill with him, yet it is well with him.

Not that we look for ill things! We are glad when all things go well with us, with our relations, and with our estates. But with the righteous man all things go well. His person is sealed; he is heir of all God's promises; he is Christ's favoured man; heaven awaits him. Is it not then well with the righteous? If you would have happiness you must espouse holiness. 'Say unto the righteous, it shall be well with him.'

So much for the first proposition: the godly man's comfort in life and death; it is well with him.

Now if all this will not prevail with you to make you leave your sins and become righteous, I must pass to the next branch of the text, to scare men out of their sins, to fright men out of their wickedness. 'Woe unto the wicked, it shall be ill with him.'

This, my beloved, is the dark side of the cloud. It may cause in every wicked man that hears me a trembling at the heart. 'Woe unto the wicked, it shall be ill with him.' The proposition that results from these words is this: When things seem to be well with the wicked, it shall be ill with them at last. Though they have more than heart can wish, yet it shall be ill with them at last. 'It shall not be well with the wicked, neither shall he prolong his days, which are as a shadow; because he feareth not before God' (*Eccles.* 8:13). The God of truth has pronounced that it shall not be well with the wicked. It is as true as God is true, 'it shall not be well with the wicked.'

That I may make this clear to you, I shall demonstrate it in four ways:

1. It is ill with the wicked in this life. A wicked man that hears me will hardly think so, when he has the affluence and confluence of outward comforts. When he eats the fat and drinks the sweet, he will hardly believe the minister who tells him that it shall be ill with him. But it is so. For is it not ill with that man that has a curse, yea, the curse of God hanging over him? Can that man thrive that lives under the curse of God? Floods of wrath hang over the head of a wicked man; he is heir to all the plagues written in the book of God. All God's curses are the sinner's portion, and if he dies in his sin, he is sure to have his portion paid him.

Woe unto the wicked! Every bit of bread he has carries with it a curse; it is like poisoned bread given to a god.

Every drop of wine he drinks, he swallows down a curse with it. Woe unto the wicked! There is a curse in his cup and a curse upon his table. God says woe unto him. We read that Belshazzar 'drank wine . . . [and] commanded to bring the golden and silver vessels which his father Nebuchadnezzar had taken out of the temple which was in Jerusalem . . . and the king and his princes, his wives, and his concubines, drank in them' (*Dan.* 5:1-3). Belshazzar was very jovial; in the midst of his cups he was merry. But woe unto the wicked! 'In the same hour came forth fingers of a man's hand, and wrote over against the candlestick upon the plaster of the wall of the king's palace . . . Then the king's countenance was changed, and his thoughts troubled him' (*Dan.* 5:5, 6) Woe was written on the wall. Let a sinner live till he come to an hundred years of age, yet he is cursed. His grey hairs have a curse on them (*Isa.* 65:20).

2. It is ill with the wicked, not only in this life, but at the hour of his death.

Death puts an end to all his comforts. No more indulging and pampering the flesh! No more cups of wine! No more music! 'The fruits that thy soul lusteth after are departed from thee' (*Rev.* 18:14). All the things that are dainty and good are departed from thee; the voice of the harper, the musician, and the trumpeter, shall be heard no more in thee. As it is spoken of the destruction of Rome, so you may say of the wicked man—no more joy and gladness, no more mirth and music. All a sinner's sweet spices, his scarlet robes, his sparkling diamonds, they all depart from him at death.

As death puts an end to a sinner's mirth, so it lays a foundation for all his sorrows. Alas, before death begins to close a sinner's eyes, the eye of his conscience is first opened. At the hour of death every sin stands with a drawn sword in its hand. Those sins that in life delighted him now affright and terrify him; all his joy and mirth turns into sadness. As sometimes you have seen how sugar lying in a damp place dissolves and runs to water: even thus at the hour of death all the sugared joys of a wicked man turn into water, into the water of tears, into the water of sorrow.

3. It shall be ill with the wicked man at the day of judgment. When he appears before God's tribunal, then he shall leave off judging others and shall stand at God's bar and be tried for his life.

I read concerning Felix that, when he heard Paul speak of judgment, he trembled. Josephus observes that Felix was a wicked man; she who lived with him—her name was Drusilla—he enticed from her husband and lived in uncleanness with her. When Felix heard Paul preaching of judgment, he trembled. Now if he trembled to hear of judgment, what will he do when judgment comes? What will he do when all his secret sins shall be made manifest, when all his midnight wickedness shall be written on his forehead, as with a point of a diamond?

At the day of judgment, there shall be a legal trial. God will call forth a sinner by name, and say, 'Stand forth, hear thy charge; see what thou canst answer to this charge! What canst thou say for thy sabbath-breaking, for thy murders, and drunkenness, and perjury? for all thy revenge and malice? for all thy persecuting of my members? What dost thou say, Guilty, or Not Guilty? Thou wretch, thou darest not say thou art not guilty; for have not I been an eye-witness to all thy wickedness? Do not the books agree—the book of thy conscience, and the book of my omniscience—and darest thou offer to plead not guilty?' How the sinner will be amazed with horror and run into desperation!

After this legal process of trial follows the sentence, 'Depart, ye cursed, into everlasting fire.' What! to go from the presence of Christ, in whose presence is fulness of joy! to go from Christ with a curse! Why, says Chrysostom, that very word 'Depart' is worse than the torment itself. And remember this, you that go on in your sins, when once this sentence is past, it cannot be reversed. This is the supreme court of judicature from which there is no appeal. Here on earth men take their causes from one court to another, from the common law to the court of chancery. But at the last day of judgment there will be no appeals against the sentence, for this is the highest court.

4. It will be ill with the wicked that die in their sins, after the day of judgment. Oh! then there will be but one way, and they would be glad they might not go that way; any way but to prison. Oh! there is no way but to hell. 'In hell he lift up his eyes' (*Luke* 16:23). Hell is the very centre of misery; it is the very distillation of the spirit of torment. The Scripture tells us that in hell there are these three things: there is darkness, there is fire, and there are chains.

Hell is called a place of darkness. 'To whom is reserved the blackness of darkness' (*Jude* 13). Darkness, you know, is the most uncomfortable thing in the world; a man that goes in the dark, he trembles at every step he takes. Hell is a black region, nothing but blackness of darkness; and it must needs be a dark place where they shall be separated from the light of God's presence. Indeed, Augustine thinks there shall be some little sulphurous light there; but suppose it be so, that light shall serve only to let the damned see the tragedy of their own misery and see themselves tormented.

And as there is darkness in hell, so there is fire; it is called a burning lake. 'Whosoever was not found written in the book of life was cast into the lake of fire' (*Rev.* 20:15). You know that fire is the most torturing element; it makes the most dreadful impression on the flesh. Now hell is a place of fire. It is disputed among the learned what kind of fire it is, and I wish we may never know what kind of fire it is. Augustine and others affirm that it is material fire, but far hotter than any fire upon your hearths; that is but painted fire compared with this. But I rather think that the fire of the damned is partly material and partly spiritual; partly material to work on the body, and partly spiritual, which is the wrath of God to torment the soul. His wrath is the lake, the burning fire. Oh! who knows the power of God's anger? Who can dwell with these burnings? It is intolerable to endure them and impossible to escape them.

In hell there are chains, 'chains of darkness' (2 *Pet.* 2:4). Those sinners that would not be bound by any law of God shall have chains of darkness to bind them. I suppose that the phrase 'chains of darkness' intimates to us that the wicked in hell shall not have power to walk up and down, which perhaps might provide a little ease, though very little. They shall be chained down fast so as not to stir; they shall be fastened to that stake with chains of darkness. Oh! this will be terrible indeed. Suppose a man should lie forever on a bed of down, unable to stir from his place, it would be very painful unto him. Oh! but to lie as the damned upon the rack, always under the torturing scorchings of God's wrath, and to be tied so as not to move, how dreadful are the thoughts of this! And this is the condition of the wicked: darkness, fire and chains!

There are two more things to show you that 'it shall be ill with the wicked,' let them die when they will. The first is the worm. There is the worm to torture the damned spirits, and this is no other than the worm of conscience; 'where their worm dieth not' (*Mark* 9:44). Oh! how dreadful will it be to have this worm! Melanchthon calls the tormenting conscience 'a hellish fury.' It will be just as if a worm full of poison were feeding upon the heart of man. Those sinners that refused to hear the voice of conscience shall feel the worm of conscience.

Secondly, as there is the worm to torment, so there is the serpent, that is, the devil, who is called the old serpent (*Rev.* 12:9). As there is the biting of the worm, so there is the stinging of the old serpent. In hell the damned shall be forced to behold the devil. I remember what Anselm says: 'I had rather endure all the torments of this life, than see the devil with bodily eyes.' But now this sight the wicked shall see whether they will or no, and not only see but they shall feel the stinging of this old serpent the devil. Satan is full of rage against mankind and will show no mercy. As he puts forth all his subtlety in tempting man, so he puts forth all his cruelty in tormenting mankind.

This is not all. These agonies and hell-convulsions shall be forever. Take that scripture, Revelation 14:11, for proof: 'And the smoke of their torment ascendeth up for ever and ever: and they have no rest day nor night.' Thus it is in hell; they would die, but they cannot. The wicked shall be always dying but never dead; the smoke of the furnace ascends forever and ever. Oh! who can endure thus to be ever upon the rack? This word 'ever' breaks the heart. Wicked men now think the sabbaths long, and say, when will the sabbath be over? They think a sermon long, and think a prayer long; but, oh! how long will it be to lie in hell for ever and ever? After millions of years their torments are as far from ended as at the first hour they began.

Another aggravation of hell torments is that the damned in hell have none to pity them. It is some comfort, some ease, to have our friends pity us in our sickness and want; aye, but those in hell have no friends. Mercy will not pity them; mercy is turned into fury. Christ will not pity them; he is no more an advocate for them. The angels will not pity them; nay, they rejoice when they see the vengeance; they exult and glory when they see the justice of God executed upon his enemies. Oh, how sad is this! to lie in the scalding furnace of God's wrath, and none to pity them! When they cry out, God will laugh at them. Oh! hear this, all ye that go into sin, 'it shall be ill with the wicked.' Oh! therefore turn from your sins, lest God tear you in pieces as a lion, and there be none to help you!

Oh! what a frightful word is this to all wicked men that go on desperately in sin and add drunkenness to thirst! Never such an inundation of wickedness as now! Men sin as if they would spite God and dare him to punish them. Men sin as greedily as if they were afraid hell gates would be shut up ere they come hither. Oh! how manfully do many sin! They go to hell strongly in their wickedness! Oh! these are in a sad condition; is it not sad with them at the hour of death, at the day of judgment, and after judgment? Wicked men live cursed, and they die damned. Sinners are the very mark that God will shoot at; they are his standing mark, and he never misses the mark. You know what the Scripture says, 'There shall be weeping, and there shall be gnashing of teeth.' Latimer says, 'That is sad fare, where weeping is the first course, and gnashing of teeth is the second.'

Whence is it that there is this gnashing of teeth?

It arises from the extremity of torment the wicked suffer; they are not able to bear it, and know not how to avoid it. Furthermore, the wicked in hell gnash their teeth at the godly to see them in heaven. They are maddened to see in heaven those whom they persecuted, and scoffed and jeered at, and themselves in hell. 'When [they] shall see Abraham, and Isaac, and Jacob, and all the prophets, in the kingdom of God, and [they themselves] shut out' (*Luke* 13:28), they shall gnash their teeth at this. Wickedness and the curse of God go hand in hand, and for the evil man there is no escape.

Take heed that none of you here be found amongst the number of the wicked. Take heed of belonging to that black regiment that wears the devil's colours and fights under his banner. The sinner and the furnace shall never be parted. Oh! take heed of those sins which will bring you to hell-fire!

Bernard says that there are fiery sins that bring men to hellfire! What are those sins? Why, the fire of malice, the fire of passion, the fire of lust and concupiscence, and the fire of revenge; these fiery sins bring men to fiery plagues, to hell-fire. When you are tempted to any wickedness, think with yourselves, 'Oh! how can I bear the fierceness of God's wrath for ever? How can I lie in the winepress of God's wrath for ever?' Oh! take heed of those sins that will bring you into this place of torment.

I have read a story of a virgin who, being tempted by a young man to commit folly, said to him, 'Grant me but one request, and I will do what you desire.' 'What is that?' said he. 'Do but hold your finger one hour in this burning candle.' But he would not do it. She said, 'Will you not for my sake hold your finger an hour in the candle, and will you have my soul lie burning in hell for ever?' Thus she rebuked the tempter.

Does Satan tempt you to wickedness? Then hold out this text as a shield to quench his fiery darts. Say thus, 'Oh, Satan! if I embrace thy temptations, I must be under thy tormenting to all eternity.' Oh! therefore labour to be righteous, for it shall be well with the righteous. But take heed of sin; it shall be ill with the sinner.

I will conclude all with that saying of Augustine: 'When a man has been virtuous, his labour is gone, but the pleasure remains; when a man has been wicked, the pleasure is gone, but the sting remains.'

PARTING COUNSELS

Having therefore these promises, dearly beloved, let us cleanse ourselves.
(2 Cor. 7:1)

What I intend now, by the help of God, to insist upon is that sweet parenthesis in the text, 'dearly beloved,' where you have the apostle breathing forth his affections unto this people. He speaks now as a pastor, and he speaks to them as his spiritual children.

In the text you have

I. The title: 'dearly beloved.'

II. The exhortation to holiness: 'Let us cleanse ourselves.'

III. The means how we should be cleansed and sanctified: 'having these promises.'

It is the first of these that I intend to speak upon, the title that the apostle gives to his children, 'dearly beloved.' From hence observe that the affections of the true gospel-minister towards his people are very ardent.

Dearly beloved, there are two things in every minister of Christ that are much exercised: his head and his heart—his head with labour and his heart with love. His head is exercised with labour in the work of the ministry. If done aright, it is a work fitter for angels than for men. It is our work to open the oracles of God, even those sacred profound things that the angels search into; and if God did not help us, we might soon sink under the weight of such a burden. And as a minister's head is exercised with labour, so his heart is exercised with love; and it is hard to say which is the greater, his labour or his love. Thus it is here in the text, 'dearly beloved.'

In these words we have St Paul laying siege to these Corinthians and labouring to make a happy victory, to conquer them with kindness. 'Dearly beloved.' St Paul's heart was the spring of love, his lips were the pipe, the Corinthians were the cistern into which this spring ran. This holy apostle was a mirror and pattern of love towards the sinning Corinthians. Paul's tears dropped towards the praying Corinthians, his love burned. Holy Paul was a seraph, his heart burned in a flame of affection to his people. How many passages do we find scattered in his epistles in which he tells his people, whom sometimes he wrote to, and sometimes he preached to, how he looked after their souls more than their silver. 'I seek not yours, but you' (2 *Cor.* 12:14). As a tender nurse cherisheth her child with the breast, so Paul gave his people the breast-milk of the Word (*1 Thess.* 2:7). This man of God not only bestowed a sermon upon his people, but was willing to impart his very soul to them if it might save theirs. 'We were willing to have imparted unto you, not the gospel of God only, but also our own souls, because ye were dear unto us' (*1 Thess.* 2:8). Such was Paul's affection to his people that he loved them more than his life: 'and if I be offered upon the sacrifice and service of your faith, I joy, and rejoice with you all' (*Phil.* 2:17). That is, as if he had said, my blood be poured forth as a sacrifice, if my death may be in any way serviceable unto you, if it may help forward the strengthening and confirming of your faith, I am willing to die, I rejoice in it. So full of affection was this apostle that he could not choose but love his people, though the more he did love, the less he should be loved (2 *Cor.* 12:15). Oh, how Paul sweetened all his sermons with love! If he reproved sin, yet he was angry in love; he dipped the pill in sugar. 'How turn ye again to the weak and beggarly elements . . . ? Ye observe days, and months, and times, and years. I am afraid of you, lest I have bestowed upon you labour in vain. Brethren, I beseech you, be as I am' (*Gal.* 4:9-11). See how Paul chides their sins and at the same time courts their souls. No sooner did he lance the wound, but immediately he poured wine and oil into it. Paul so loved his people that he would not justly give any offence to the weakest believer. 'If meat make my brother to offend, I will eat no flesh while the world standeth' (*1 Cor.* 8:13). Paul was like some tender mother, who forbears to eat those foods that she might, for fear of hurting the child that she gives suck to. Thus you see he was a spiritual father, made up of love. And surely, my brethren, this affection in some degree is in all the true ministers of Jesus Christ.

They are full of sympathy and affection towards those over whom the Holy Ghost has made them overseers.

One reason why there *will* be in all Christ's ministers such flaming affections to their people is that principle within them that teaches love. Grace does not fire the heart with passion, but with compassion. Grace in the heart of a minister files off that ruggedness that is in his spirit, making him loving and courteous. Paul once breathed out persecution, but when grace came this bramble was turned into a spiritual vine, twisting himself about the souls of his people with loving embraces.

This ardent love will also be in a minister's heart because of that spiritual relation that is betwixt him and his people. He is a spiritual father, and shall we think him to be without feeling? 'Though ye have ten thousand instructors in Christ, yet have ye not many fathers: for in Christ Jesus I have begotten you through the gospel' (*1 Cor.* 4:15). Some he begets unto Christ, others he builds up in Christ. Does not a father provide cheerfully for his children? Can a father see bread taken from his child, and not have his heart affected with it? Is it not a grief to a parent to see his child put to a dry nurse?

There *should* be this ardent love and affection in all God's ministers because this is the liveliest way to do most good. Knotty and stubborn hearts will soonest be wrought upon with kindness. Fire melts the hardest metal; and the fire of love, with God's blessing, will melt the most obdurate sinner. A Barnabas, a son of consolation, who comes in the spirit of love and meekness, is the fittest to do a piece of gospel-surgery to restore and put such a one in joint again that is overtaken with a fault. 'Restore such an one in the spirit of meekness' (*Gal.* 6:1). So much in short for the doctrinal parts.

Give me leave now to make some application. The first thing we see here is the true character of a gospel-minister. He is full of love; he exhorts, he comforts, he reproves, and all in love. He is never angry with his people except when they will not be saved. How loth is a minister of Christ to see precious souls like so many jewels cast over-board into the dead-sea of hell. A conscientious minister would count it an unhappy gain to gain the world and lose the souls of his people. He says, as the King of Sodom to Abraham, 'Give me the persons, and take the goods to thyself' (*Gen.* 14:21).

The second thing to learn is this. If true gospel-ministers are so full of love, how sad it is to have such ministers put upon a people as have no love for their souls. The work of the ministry is a labour of love. Oh, how sad it is to have in the ministry such as can neither labour nor love, such as are without affections, that look more at tithes than at souls. It must needs be sad with a people in any part of the world to have such ministers set over them as either poison them with error or do what in them lies to damn them by their wicked example. How can the devil reprove sin? How can the minister cry out in the pulpit against drunkenness, who will himself be drunk? 'Thou that preachest a man should not steal, dost thou steal? Thou that sayest a man should not commit adultery, dost thou commit adultery?' (*Rom.* 2:21, 22). We read that the snuffers of the tabernacle were to be made of pure gold (*Exod.* 37:23). Those who by their calling are to reprove and snuff off the sins of others should be pure gold, holy persons. In the law God appointed that the lip of the leper should be covered (*Lev.* 13:45). Neither should he be permitted to speak the oracles of God, who though he is by office an angel, yet by life is a leper.

The third thing we learn is the happiness of a minister who is placed among such a people as give him abundant cause of love. How happy is he that can say to his people from his heart, 'My dearly beloved'; and here let me speak by way of encouragement to you of this parish. I find the apostle commending the good he saw in his people: 'We are bound to thank God always for you, brethren, because that your faith groweth exceedingly' (2 *Thess.* 1:3). Here Paul is commending his people. In imitation of the apostle, let me at this time speak a commendatory word to you. I have exercised my ministry now among you for almost sixteen years, and I rejoice and bless God that I cannot say, 'The more I love you, the less I am loved.' I have received many signal demonstrations of love from you; though other parishes have exceeded you in number of houses, yet I think not in strength of affection. I have with much comfort observed your reverent attention to the Word preached; you have rejoiced in this light not for a season, but until this day. I have observed your zeal against error, and as much as could be expected in a critical time, your unity and amity. This is your honour; and if for the future there should be any interruption made in my ministry among you, though I should not be permitted to preach to you, yet I shall not cease to love you and to pray for you. But why should there be any interruption made? Where is the crime? Some indeed say that we are disloyal and seditious. Beloved, what my actings and sufferings for His Majesty have been is known to not a few of you. However, we must go to heaven through good report and bad report, and it is well if we can get glory, though we pass through the pikes. I shall endeavour to prove the sincerity of my love to you. I will not promise that I shall still preach among you, nor will I say that I shall not. I desire to be guided by the silver thread of God's Word and of God's providence. My heart is toward you.

There is, you know, an expression in the late Act that shortly we should be as if we were naturally dead; and, if I must die, let me leave some legacy with you before I go from you. I cannot but give you some counsel and advice for your souls, and I hope there is no hurt in that. There are, my beloved, these twenty directions, that I desire you to take special notice of, which I would leave as advice and counsel with you about your souls.

1. I beseech you, keep your constant hours every day with God. The godly man is a man 'set apart' (*Psa.* 4:3), not only because God has set him apart by election, but because he has set himself apart by devotion. Begin the day with God, visit God in the morning before you make any other visit. Wind up your hearts toward heaven in the morning, and they will go the better all the day after. Oh, turn your houses into temples. Read the Scriptures. The two Testaments are the two lips by

which God speaks to us; these will make you wise unto salvation. The Scripture is both a glass to show you your spots and a laver to wash them away. Besiege heaven every day with prayer; thus perfume your houses, and keep a constant intercourse with heaven.

2. Get good books in your houses. When you have not the spring near to you, then get water into your cistern; so when you have not that wholesome preaching that you desire, good books are cisterns that hold the waters of life in them to refresh you. When David's natural heat was taken away, they covered him with warm clothes (*1 Kings* 1:1); so when you find a chilliness upon your souls and your former heat begins to abate, ply yourselves with warm clothes, get those good books that may acquaint you with such truths as may warm and affect your hearts.

3. Have a care of your company. Take heed of unnecessary familiarity with sinners. We cannot catch health from another, but we may soon catch a disease; the disease of sin is very catching. I would be as afraid of coming among the wicked as among those that have the plague. They 'were mingled among the heathen, and learned their works' (*Psa.* 106:35). If we cannot make others better, let us have a care that they do not make us worse. Lot was a miracle, he kept fresh in Sodom's salt water. My beloved, take heed of the occasions of sin; evil company is an occasion of sin. The Nazarites in the old law, as they might drink no wine, so they were forbidden grapes, whereof the wine was made (*Num.* 6:3, 4). This was to teach us that all occasions of sin must be

avoided. Evil company is the devil's draw-net, by which he draws millions to hell. How many families and how many souls have been ruined and undone in this city by evil company! Many there are that go from a playhouse to a whorehouse, and from a tavern to Tyburn.[1]

4. Have a care whom you hear. It is our Saviour Christ's counsel; 'Beware of false prophets, which come to you in sheep's clothing, but inwardly they are ravening wolves' (*Matt.* 7:15). Let me tell you, the devil has his ministers as well as Christ. 'The serpent cast out of his mouth water as a flood after the woman' (*Rev.* 12:15), that is, as the learned expound it, Satan by his ministers and emissaries cast out the flood of Arian doctrine to drown the church. There are some who by the subtlety of their wit have learned the art to mix error with truth and to give poison in a golden cup. Take heed who you hear and how you hear. Be like those Bereans that searched the Scriptures whether the things that they heard preached were so or not (*Acts* 17:11). Your ears must not be like sponges that suck in puddle water as well as wine, but your ears must be like a fan that fans out the chaff but retains the pure wheat. You must be like those in the parable who gathered the good fish into vessels but cast the bad away (*Matt.* 13:48). The saints are called virgins for their wisdom; they will not let anyone defile their souls with error. They have a judicious ear and a critical palate that can distinguish between truth and error, and they put a difference between meat of God's sending and the devil's cooking.

[1] Tyburn was the location of the public gallows.—P.

5. Follow after sincerity: 'Behold, thou desirest truth in the inward parts' (*Psa.* 51:6). Be what you seem to be. Do not be like rowers in a boat that look one way and row another. Do not look heavenward by your profession and row hell-ward by your practice. Do not pretend to love God, and yet love sin. Counterfeit piety is double iniquity. Let your hearts be upright with God. The plainer the diamond is, the richer it is; and the more plain the heart is, the more does God value his jewel. A little rusty gold is far better than a great deal of bright brass; a little true grace, though rusted over with many infirmities, is better than all the glittering shows of hypocrites. A sincere heart is God's current coin.

6. As you love your souls, be not strangers to yourselves. Be much and often in the work of self-examination. Among all the books that you read, turn over the book of your own heart; look into the book of conscience; see what is written there. 'I commune with mine own heart' (*Psa.* 77:6). Set up a judgment seat in your own souls; examine whether you have grace or not; prove whether you are in the faith. Be as much afraid of a painted holiness as you would be afraid of going to a painted heaven. Do not think yourselves good because others think so. Let the Word be the touchstone by which you try your hearts. Let the Word be the looking-glass by which you judge the complexion of your souls. For want of this self-searching, many live known to others and die unknown to themselves.

7. Keep your spiritual watch. 'What I say unto you I say unto all, Watch' (*Mark* 13:37). If it were the last

word I should speak, it should be this word, Watch! Oh, what need has a Christian to be ever upon his watch! The heart is a subtle piece, and will be stealing out to vanity, and if we are not careful, it will decoy us into sin. We have a special eye upon such persons as we suspect: your heart is a suspicious person; Oh, have an eye upon it, watch it continually, it is a bosom-traitor. Job set a watch before his eyes (*Job* 31:1). We must every day keep sentinel; sleep not upon your guard. Our sleeping time is the devil's tempting time. Let not your watch-candle go out.

8. You that are the people of God, often associate together. 'They that feared the LORD spake often one to another' (*Mal.* 3:16). Christ's doves should flock together. One Christian will help to heat another: a single coal of juniper will soon die, but many coals put together will keep life in one another. Conference sometimes may do as much good as preaching. One Christian by good discourse drops holy oil upon another, which makes the lamp of his grace to shine the brighter. It is great wisdom to keep a company's trade on the move. Christians by meeting often together, setting good discourse on foot, keep up the trade of godliness that otherwise would decay and soon be lost. Is not the communion of saints an article in our creed? Do not then live so asunder, as if this article were blotted out. The naturalists observe there is a sympathy in plants; they say some plants bear better when they grow near other plants. The vine and the elm, the olive and the myrtle thrive best when they grow together.

Similarly, it is true in religion; the saints are trees of righteousness. They thrive best in godliness when they grow together.

9. Get your hearts screwed up above the world, 'Set your affection on things above' (*Col.* 3:2). We may see the face of the moon in water, but the moon is fixed above in the firmament; so though a Christian walk here below, yet his heart should be fixed above in heaven. In heaven is our best kindred, our purest joy, our mansion-house. Oh, let our hearts be above; it is the best and the sweetest kind of life. The higher the bird flies, the sweeter it sings; and the higher the heart is raised above the world, the sweeter joy it has. The eagle that flies in the air is not stung by the serpent. Those whose hearts are elevated above the lower region of this world are not stung with the vexations and disquietments that others experience, but are full of joy and contentments.

10. Trade much in the promises. The promises are great supports to faith; faith lives in a promise, as the fish lives in water. The promises are both comforting and quickening, they are the very breasts of the gospel; as the child by sucking the breasts gets strength, so faith by sucking the breast of a promise gets strength and revives. The promises of God are bladders to keep us from sinking when we come into the waters of affliction. The promises are sweet clusters of grapes that grow upon Christ the true vine. Oh, trade much in the promises! There is no condition that you can be in, but you have a promise. The promises are like manna that suit themselves to every Christian's palate.

11. To all you that hear me, live in a calling. Jerome advised his friend to be ever well employed, that when the devil came to tempt him, he might find him working in God's vineyard. Sure I am that the same God who says, 'Remember the sabbath day, to keep it holy,' also says, 'Six days shalt thou labour.' The great God never sealed any warrants for idleness. An idle professor is the shame of his profession. 'We hear that there are some which walk among you disorderly, working not at all, but are busybodies. Now them that are such we command and exhort by our Lord Jesus Christ, that with quietness they work' (2 *Thess.* 3:11, 12). Solon made laws to punish idleness; and Cicero says of an idle man, 'he draws his breath, but does not live.' An idle man is useless; but a good Christian acts within the sphere of his own calling.

12. Let me entreat you to join the first and second tables of the law together, piety to God, and equity to your neighbour. The apostle put these two words together in one verse (*Titus* 2:12), that 'we should live . . . righteously, and godly': righteously, that relates to morality; godly, that relates to piety and sanctity. Always remember this, every command has the same divine stamp and authority as another command has. I would test a moral man by the duties of the first table, and I would test a professing Christian by the duties of the second table. Some pretend to faith, but have no works; others have works, but they have no faith. Some pretend to zeal for God, but are not just in their dealings; others are just in their dealings, but have not one

spark of zeal for God. If you would go to heaven, you must run both sides of the table, the first and second table. Join piety and morality together. As we blame the Papists for blotting out the second commandment, let not the Papists blame us for leaving out the second table.

13. Join the serpent and the dove together, innocence and prudence (*Matt.* 10:16): 'Be . . . wise as serpents, and harmless as doves.' We must have innocence with our wisdom, else our wisdom is but craftiness; and we must have wisdom with our innocence, else our innocence is but weakness. We must have the harmlessness of the dove, that we may not wrong others; and we must have the prudence of the serpent, that others may not abuse and circumvent us. Not to wrong the truth by silence—here is the innocence of the dove. Not to betray ourselves by rashness—here is the wisdom of the serpent. How happy it is where these two are united, the dove and the serpent. The dove without the serpent is folly, and the serpent without the dove is impiety.

14. Be more afraid of sin than of suffering. A man may be afflicted, and yet have the love of God; but if he sin, immediately God is angry. Sin eclipses the light of God's countenance. In suffering, the conscience may be quiet. When the hail beats upon the tiles, there may be music in the house; and when there is suffering in the body, there may be peace and music in the conscience. But when a man sins wilfully and presumptuously, he loses all his peace. Francis Spira abjured his faith, and he became a terror to himself; he could not endure himself;

he professed he thought Cain and Judas in hell did not feel those terrors and horrors that he felt. He that will commit sin to prevent suffering, is like a man that lets his head be wounded to save his shield and helmet.

15. Take heed of idolatry. 'Little children, keep yourselves from idols' (*1 John* 5:21). Idolatry is an image of jealousy to provoke God. It breaks the marriage knot asunder and makes the Lord disclaim his interest in a people. What kind of religion is popery? It is the mother of many monsters. What soul-damning doctrines does it hold forth, as the meriting of salvation by good works, the giving of pardons, the worshipping of angels, popish indulgences, purgatory, and the like. It is a soul-damning religion; it is the breeder of ignorance, uncleanness and murder. The popish religion is not defended by strength of argument, but by force of arms. Keep yourselves from idols and take heed of superstition; that is the gentleman-usher to popery.

16. Think not the worse of godliness because it is reproached and persecuted. Wicked men, being stirred up by the devil, maliciously reproach the ways of God. Such were Julian and Lucian. Though wicked men would be godly on their deathbeds, yet in the time of their life they revile and hate godliness. But do not think the worse of religion because it is reproached by the wicked. Suppose a virgin should be reproached for her chastity, yet chastity is none the worse; if a blind man jeer at the sun, the sun is none the less bright. Holiness is a beautiful and glorious thing; it is the angels' glory, and shall we be ashamed of that which makes us like the

angels? There is a time coming when wicked men will be glad of some of that holiness that now they despise, but they shall be as far then from obtaining it as they are now from desiring it.

17. Think not the better of sin because it is in fashion. Think not the better of impiety and ungodliness because many walk in those crooked ways. Multitude is a foolish argument; multitude does not argue the goodness of a thing. The devil's name is Legion, which signifies a multitude. Hell-road is this day full of travellers. Esteem not sin the better, because most go this way. Do we think the better of the plague because it is common? The plea of a multitude will not hold out at God's bar when God shall ask you, Why did you profane my sabbath? Why were you drunk? Why did you break your oath? To say then, Lord, because most men did so, will be but a poor plea; God will say to you, Then seeing you have sinned with the multitude, you shall now go to hell with the multitude. I beseech you as you care for your souls, walk antipodes to the corruptions of the times. If you are living fish, swim against the stream; dead fish swim down the stream. 'Have no fellowship with the unfruitful works of darkness, but rather reprove them' (*Eph.* 5:11).

18. In the business of religion serve God with all your might. 'Whatsoever thy hand findeth to do, do it with thy might, for there is no work, nor device . . . in the grave, whither thou goest' (*Eccles.* 9:10). This is an argument why we should do all we can for God. We should serve him with all our strength because the grave is very near,

and there is no praying, no repenting in the grave. Our time is but small, and therefore our zeal for God should be great. David danced with all his might before the ark, and so should we act vigorously for God in the sphere of obedience. 'Fervent in spirit; serving the Lord' (*Rom.* 12:11). Take heed of a dull, lazy temper in God's service. You must not only say a prayer or read a prayer, but you must pour out your soul in prayer. You must not only love God, but be 'sick of love' to God. God in the old law would have the coals put to the incense (*Lev.* 16:13), and why so? To typify that the heart must be inflamed in the worship of God; your prayers must go up with a flame of devotion. I confess hell will be taken without storm; you may jump into hell with ease. But it is all uphill to heaven, and therefore you must put forth all your might. 'The violent take it by force' (*Matt.* 11:12). Heaven is not taken but by storm. Do you see men zealous and very active for hell, and will you not take pains for heaven?

19. Do all the good you can to others as long as you live. God has made every creature useful for us; the sun has not its light for itself, but for us; the fountain runs freely, and the myrrh drops freely from the tree. Every creature does as it were deny itself; the beast gives us its labour, the bird gives us its music, and the silkworm its silk. Now has God made everything useful for us, and shall not we be useful one for another? Oh, labour to be helpful to the souls of others and to supply the wants of others. Jesus Christ was a public blessing in the world; he went about doing good. We are all members

of the body politic, nay, are we not members of the body mystical, and shall not every member be helpful for the good of the body? That is a dead member that does not contribute to the good of the body. Oh, labour to be useful to others while you live, so that when you die, you may be missed. Many live so unfruitfully, that truly their life is scarce worth a prayer, nor their death scarce worth a tear.

20. Every day think upon eternity. Oh, eternity, eternity! All of us here are, ere long—it may be some of us within a few days or hours—to launch forth into the ocean of eternity. Eternity is 'endless duration,' says Eoetius; no prospective-glass can see to the end of eternity. Eternity is a sum that can never be numbered, a line that can never be measured. Eternity is a condition of everlasting misery or everlasting happiness. If you are godly then shall you be for ever happy, you shall be always sunning yourselves in the light of God's countenance. If you are wicked, you shall be always miserable, ever lying in the scalding furnace of the wrath of the Almighty. Eternity to the godly is a day that has no sunset; eternity to the wicked is a night that has no sunrise. Oh, I beseech you, my brethren, every day spend some time thinking upon eternity. The serious thoughts of an eternal condition would be a great means to promote holiness.

The thoughts of eternity would make us very serious about our souls. Oh, my soul, you are shortly to fly into eternity, a condition that can never be reversed or altered. How serious would this make us about our heaven-born souls! Zenxes being asked why he was so long in drawing a picture, answered, 'I am now painting for eternity.' Oh, how fervently would that man pray that thinks he is praying for eternity. Oh, how accurately and circumspectly would that man live who thinks that upon this moment hangs eternity.

The thoughts of eternity would make us slight and contemn all the things of this world. What is the world to him that has eternity always in his eye? Did we think seriously and solemnly of eternity, we should never over-value the comforts of the world, nor over-grieve at the crosses of the world.

We should not over-value the comforts of the world. Worldly comforts are very sweet, but they are very swift; they are soon gone. The pleasures of the world are but for a season, just like Noah's dove that brought an olive branch in her mouth, but she had wings, and so did soon fly from the ark; so are all outward comforts, they bring an olive branch, but they have wings too, with which they fly away.

The thoughts of eternity would keep us from grieving overmuch at crosses and sufferings of the world. Our sufferings, says the apostle, are but for a while. What are all the sufferings we can undergo in the world in comparison with eternity? Affliction may be lasting, but it is not everlasting. Our sufferings here are not worthy to be compared to an eternal weight of glory.

And thus, my beloved, I have given you these twenty directions for your precious souls. I beseech you treasure them up as so many jewels in the cabinet of your breast.

If you carry these directions about with you, they will be a most excellent antidote to keep you from sin, and an excellent means to preserve the zeal of piety flaming upon the altar of your hearts.

I have many things yet to say to you, but I know not whether God will give me another opportunity; my strength is now almost gone. I beseech you, let these things which I have spoken make deep impressions upon all your souls. Consider what has been said, and the Lord give you understanding in all things.

JOHN OLDFIELD

LIFE

John Oldfield, born near Chesterfield, Derbyshire, about 1627, was educated at the grammar school of Bromfield in Cumberland. Although he did not proceed to university, he was regarded as an accomplished scholar. Oldfield was appointed to the rectory of Carsington, Derbyshire, about 1649, later refusing the offer of a better-paid living at Tamworth. The people at Carsington, who were notoriously hard to please, held him in great affection. From 1651-8 a classis[1] of ministers met regularly at Wirksworth, of which he was an active member. Oldfield was noted for his moderate spirit, and, when the Act of Uniformity was passed, decided that he could not conform only after long and serious consideration.

After being ejected, Oldfield moved from place to place, finally settling at Alfreton, Derbyshire. Though not averse to attending the established church, he preached frequently in conventicles, and in 1672 was licensed under the Declaration of Indulgence at a house in Road Nook. There he preached every fortnight. Oldfield died

[1] That is, a governing body of pastors and elders.—P.

in 1682 and was buried at Alfreton. Twice married, he had four sons who followed him in the ministry, the eldest conforming to the Church of England. His published works include a tract against hypocrisy entitled *The First Last and the Last First* and a treatise on prayer, *The Generation of Seekers*.

STUMBLING AT THE SUFFERINGS OF THE GODLY

Let not them that wait on thee, O Lord God of hosts, be ashamed for my sake: let not those that seek thee be confounded for my sake, O God of Israel.
Psalm 69:6

This psalm, for the main substance of it, is David's prayer for deliverance from the grievous oppression of his cruel enemies. Many passages in it also have respect to Christ (of whom David was an eminent type) and part of the 9th verse is applied to him in John 2:17 and the rest of it in Romans 15:3. Many more passages in it are also applied to Christ.

This petition in our text for deliverance (whether you refer it to David or Christ) is propounded in the beginning of the first verse, 'Save me.' It is prosecuted and urged with divers arguments, the first being drawn from the greatness of the calamity under which he lay (verses 1, 2), the second from his long waiting and earnest crying, his throat dried, his eyes fail (verse 3), the third from the number and nature of his enemies, more than the hairs of his head, and they very malicious and injurious, hating him causelessly, forcing him to unjust restitution; under which also is couched a fourth argument, *viz.*, his own innocency in the matter of which he was accused, and for which he was hated and persecuted (verse 4).

Notwithstanding this innocency of his as to the particulars with which he was charged by men, he yet justifies God in permitting these evils to befall him; for this I take to be part of the sense of the 5th verse: 'O God, thou knowest my foolishness'—and therefore I cannot justify myself before thee, nor accuse thee of injustice for permitting it to be thus with me. Though the words may seem also to look another way, *viz.*, to be David's appeal to God concerning his innocency in those particulars—'Thou, Lord, who knowest my foolishness, from whom my sins are not hid, knowest my innocency in the things whereof I am accused.'

Take note that when men oppress and persecute most unjustly, yet there is cause to justify God in suffering it to be so. God's justice is executed upon us by their injustice; if men falsely accuse us, yet God can truly charge us. When Job had to deal with men, he maintains his integrity against their accusations (*Job.* 27:4-6), but when he has to deal with God, he acknowledges his sin and will not stand upon his own justification; he will not plead, but supplicate (*Job* 9). The prophet Jeremiah grants the conclusion (*Jer.* 12:1), though he desires to debate with God about the prosperity of the wicked and about God's permitting them to oppress and trample upon his people. If any of God's people think they have hard measure from men, that they are wrongfully and injuriously handled as to some particular, yet let them eye God and consider their carriage towards him, and they shall find cause enough to say, as Ezra, 'Thou . . . hast punished us less than our iniquities deserve' (*Ezra* 9:13). It may seem hard that the poor messengers of Christ, who desire nothing more but liberty to speak to souls that they might be saved and have daily bread, should be deprived of this liberty and livelihood upon such grounds as were not necessary to be imposed by others, to which they cannot submit without losing the peace of their conscience and credit of their ministry. Yet who is so innocent that he cannot see reason enough to justify God? Alas, there is so much unfaithfulness, lukewarmness, negligence, laziness, and a thousand other miscarriages to be found in us as may abundantly justify God in this dispensation, though he seem to spit in our faces and to lay us aside as a vessel in which he has no pleasure.

But to come to the text. It may be considered with relation to what goes before and to the scope of the psalm; and so it is an argument enforcing the petition for deliverance, drawn from the ill consequence which would follow if God should permit his enemies thus to insult, *viz.*, that hereby the godly would be ashamed and confounded, they would stumble and take offence at his sufferings. Or it may be considered absolutely, and so the text is a petition that God would prevent that sad consequence of his sufferings by his seasonable deliverance or some other way.

In the words thus considered, observe:

1. To whom the petition is directed, *viz.*, to God, described by a double title, the one of majesty, 'Lord God of Hosts'; the other of mercy, 'God of Israel.'

2. For whom it is made, and that is the godly, described by a double practice of theirs, *viz.*, those that wait on God and those that seek him.

3. The matter of the petition, and that is, that such might not be ashamed and confounded.

4. The motive that induced him to make this petition, or that which gave occasion of it, and that is included in those words 'for my sake' or, as in the Hebrew, 'in me': that is, because of my grievous sufferings and calamities. The words are plain and need no further opening.

Divers observations would arise from each branch, but I shall only name three.

I. God's people are waiters on and seekers of God. This I pass by.

II. The long and grievous afflictions of God's eminent servants are apt to stumble and confound others, even the truly godly.

III. A gracious soul fears and prays against the evil influence that his sufferings might have upon others.

The second of these is what I chiefly aim at, in prosecution of which I shall first show that it is so; secondly, show what it is that men stumble at in the saints' sufferings; and, thirdly, whence it comes to pass.

First I shall show that the long and grievous afflictions of God's eminent servants are apt to stumble and confuse others, even the truly godly. That this is so, Scripture abundantly bears witness, and experience confirms.

Did not Job's friends sadly stumble at his sufferings? They were not ashamed of and confounded at him, yet they censured and condemned him for an hypocrite, as appears in their debates with him. Similarly Asaph was well-nigh gone, and had almost slipped at the consideration of his own sufferings, and the wicked's prosperity (*Psa.* 73:2, 13, 14). He declares that others were stumbled upon the same account, even 'his people' (verse 10), i.e. the people of God. But what need we multiply instances when we have one instead of all, *viz.*, the sufferings of Christ himself; at which not only others, but even his disciples and apostles themselves did sadly stumble? Peter denies and forswears him; others of them stagger and question whether he was (what he had declared himself) the redeemer of Israel (*Luke* 24:21). All forsake him; the sword awakes against the shepherd, and the sheep are scattered (*Zech.* 13:7). Thus it has been in all ages of the church. Though I deny not that the blood of the martyrs has been the seed of the church, yet that seed has not sprung up ordinarily till following ages. As for that present age in which they suffered, their falling into troubles did cause others to fall off and depart from them. The cross has been, and will be, a stone of stumbling and a rock of offence to many. Men will shun that way in which they see others plunged and sticking in the mire. Therefore has the Holy Ghost said much for the prevention of this mischief. This seems to be the scope of Psalms 37 and 73. To this purpose are recorded both dreadful threatening against those that should be ashamed of Christ or his members in their sufferings, such as Mark 8:38, and also precious promises to those that should boldly own, and openly profess him (*Matt.* 10:32, *Luke* 12:8). The Word intimates that there is a propensity in the best of men to fall into that sin. Hence it is that the apostle cautions his Thessalonians that none of them should be moved by his afflictions (*1 Thess.* 3:3).

Let me only subjoin this here (which I desire you to carry along with you through my whole discourse) that all do not stumble in the same way. Some are weakened and discouraged and so either fall off or play Nicodemus's part. Others having promised themselves a fair gale of prosperity that should waft them over safely and speedily to the heavenly shore, when they see others tossed with a Euroclydon,[1] conflicting with the winds and waves, ready to be swallowed up, or dashed in pieces upon the rocks of affliction, they make a retreat, resolving to venture no further upon that tempestuous sea; so it was with Demas and others in Paul's time. Some again stumble by passing hard censures upon those whom they see to meet with hard measures in the world. In these and divers other ways that we shall occasionally touch upon (though the text points chiefly at one way) do men stumble at the sufferings of the godly.

Let us enquire what it is that men stumble at in reference to the godly's sufferings, and we shall find chiefly three things, all of which may be fairly implied in the text.

Sometimes men (even the godly) stumble at the persons so afflicted and are ready to think hardly of them

[1] See Acts 27:14.

(as Job's friends of him) because God deals hardly with them. How common is it for men to pass harsh censures upon those that fall under heavy afflictions! and there is good reason, for there is upon every man's heart an indelible impress of God's vindictive justice. They know the judgment of God (*Rom.* 1:32), and that he is the judge of the world, to inflict punishments on offenders. They know also that this righteous judge cannot and will not pervert judgment. Hence they conclude that those so severely and signally punished must needs be guilty of some grievous enormities or monstrous impiety. A clear instance we have in the censure those barbarians passed upon Paul, when they saw the viper leap and fasten upon his hand (*Acts* 28:3, 4). Now as this impression of the divine justice remains upon the godly (as being indeed a part of their sanctification), they sometimes forget that afflictions are the portion of God's people, and that they are part of the child's portion, and so are ready to judge those to be none of God's children who are thus afflicted. Nor do men this way only stumble at the persons of the godly in afflictions, but (which is more common) they are shy of owning them. They stand at a distance from them, and forsake them (see *Psa.* 69:8, 2 *Tim.* 4:16). This was our Saviour's own case (*Isa.* 52:14; 53:2, 3). All in Asia, even Phygellus and Hermogenes turned away from Paul (2 *Tim.* 1:15). Onesiphorus is almost the only man who was not ashamed of his chain (verse 16). It is so in any kind of affliction.

But one of the saddest kinds of stumbling in this respect is when those that should be comforters turn censurers, when the godly join with the wicked in censuring their afflicted brethren, as suffering out of obstinancy and perverseness, because their consciences are not of the same latitude with their own: yet how common it is! If the conscience of a poor Christian has a more quick and lively sense of human impositions, is more tender of violating oaths, of corrupting God's worship by men's traditions, of doing things that are doubtful or that carry in them an appearance of evil; no matter how patiently he sits down under his sufferings, yet he shall be whispered about as an ignorant, scrupulous and obstinate fool, even by those who profess to own the power of godliness, though in these respects taking to themselves a greater latitude, both for their principles and practice. This, Oh, this (next to the sense of God's wrath) is one of the bitterest ingredients in the cup of the godly man's afflictions; yet he often meets with it. And against this we may reasonably think that David prays in the text, *viz.*, that the godly might neither censure nor be ashamed of him because of his sufferings.

Sometimes men stumble at the way and profession of the godly. They take up hard thoughts even of godliness itself, when it goes hard with the godly. Thus Asaph because of his own sufferings began to think his piety vain (*Psa.* 73:13). Though the Word has expressly told us that we must through many tribulations enter into the kingdom of God, and men in the general believe it, yet when sufferings befall themselves or others for holiness' sake, they forget the Word that speaks to them as to children (*Heb.* 12:6). They conclude that that is not the right way which is strewn with so many crosses, and therefore turn away from it. Hence David says, 'The rod of the wicked shall not rest upon the lot of the righteous; lest the righteous put forth their hands unto iniquity' (*Psa.* 125:3). Even the righteous are apt, by long and grievous afflictions, to be turned out of the way of righteousness, and to 'turn aside unto crooked ways' (verse 5). Therefore God will take care to prevent it, by a seasonable deliverance of his people. How many have turned their backs on Christ, when they have seen others carrying his cross upon their shoulders! The story of that King of Morocco is sufficiently known, who would not be baptized into the Christian faith because he saw many poor and ragged creatures who, he was told, were the servants of Christ. Men will shun that route upon the sea where they meet with many pieces of ships split upon the rocks; nor will they take up a calling, the professors of which are generally poor and beggarly. Doubtless the sufferings of the godly occasion in many a prejudice against godliness, in some a turning from it. Against this therefore we may rationally conclude David to pray in the text, *viz.*, that as none might misjudge his person, so neither his profession, because of his afflictions.

Sometimes men stumble at the weaknesses of the godly in their afflictions. If they see them never so little despond, or faint, or anyway waver (not considering the greatness of their troubles, nor allowing those concessions they ought to human infirmity), a cowardly carriage or an act of slavish fear or sinful compliance in a godly man becomes to them an occasion of stumbling.

There is indeed a scandal given in such miscarriages, which is the great sin of those that give it, yet others should be careful not to take it. Offences of this nature will come, while men are men, encompassed with human infirmities; but blessed are they that are not offended at such things. Some such thing is intimated in that proverb of Solomon. 'A righteous man falling down before the wicked is as a troubled fountain, and a corrupt spring' (*Prov.* 25:26). A learned commentator gives this sense. A righteous man falling down, that is, one that is drawn or driven from his duty by the flatteries or threats of the wicked, such a one is like a troubled fountain or corrupt spring that is hurtful to others. As a poisoned fountain is a public mischief, for it poisons all the streams that issue from it and all those that drink of it, so the miscarriages of such persons stumble and offend many, grieve some, and pervert others. When a pillar of the church is shaken, it must needs unsettle those that lean upon it. Such a one was Peter, and you know that not only the Jews, but even Barnabas himself was drawn away with his dissimulation (*Gal.* 2:9-13). This then may be the sense of David's petition in the text. Lord, let me not by any weakness or despondent behaviour cast a stumblingblock before them that fear thee. The sense of the petition is well expressed in the metrical psalm:

Let no man doubt, or shrink away,
for ought that chanceth me.

Thus you see what men are apt to stumble at in reference to the sufferings of the godly.

Let us enquire whence it is that men are thus apt to stumble, what may be the reason of it. The first is that carnal tenderness and sinful self-love that is deeply rooted in every man's nature. Men are loth to undergo hardships themselves, and therefore take up hard thoughts and sinister opinions of those that do. The flesh shrinks at sufferings, and therefore they shrink from those that suffer, lest they should be necessitated to suffer with them. From this principle it was that Peter dissuaded our Saviour from suffering (*Matt.* 16:22), as appears by our Saviour's reply (verses 24, 25), 'If any man will come after me, let him deny himself, and take up his cross and follow me.' I perceive, Peter, what you are driving at; 'tis care of yourself more than of me that suggests this counsel. You would not have me lead in sufferings, lest you should be compelled to follow; but I tell you, it must be so. Both you and all others that will follow me must take up their cross. It is hard to drag the carcass to the prison, to the rack, to the flames; therefore men (though otherwise good) are willing to think those in an error, or else too heady and rash in owning the truth, who expose themselves to sufferings, especially upon the account of some smaller truth. If they should conclude such to be in the right, they must needs voyage in the same ship and run the same hazard. Hence the flesh, for its own security, finds some fault in those forward sufferers with which to cloak its own backwardness.

This stumbling at the sufferings of the godly proceeds from want of due consideration of what the Word of God speaks as to the state of the godly. The Word is very plain and positive. Christ has not spoken as an imposter, but has told us the worst, as well as the best, of Christianity (*Matt.* 16:25). He has told us of forsaking houses and lands, of being delivered up to councils, scourged, cast out of the synagogues, brought before governors, and so on (*Matt.* 10:17, *Acts* 14:22, 2 *Tim.* 3:12). Yet when it comes to it indeed, we do not so seriously consider these things, nor remember them, either as to our own or others sufferings, as we ought. This was the case of the apostles when our Saviour suffered. He had expressly foretold them of his sufferings (*Matt.* 16:21), yet they were slow of heart to believe, which he upbraids them with (*Luke* 24:25, 26). Compare Matthew 17:22, 23, where he tells them, 'The Son of man shall be betrayed . . . And they were exceeding sorry,' with Luke 9:44, 45, where he tells them the same thing, and 'they understood not this saying, and it was hid from them, that they perceived it not.' How shall we reconcile these texts? The one tells you 'they were exceeding sorry'; the other, 'they understood it not.' I deny not but they may relate to different occasions, for our Saviour did often inculcate this upon them; yet methinks this may be the sense. They did understand his words and the meaning of them and were thereupon affected with some present flitting sorrow; but those things did not (as our Saviour bids they should, *Luke* 9:44) sink down into their ears. They did not, as Mary, lay them up and ponder them in their hearts. The effects these things had upon them were but like the effects of some romantic tragedy that excites some present affections, but leaves no lasting impressions; so that when Christ came to suffer, these things were as much out of their thoughts as if they had never been spoken. They had such deeply-rooted expectations of Christ's earthly kingdom that they forgot all he spoke of his death and sufferings. Thus it is, too often, a notion indeed we have that sufferings are the lot of God's children, but we are woefully wanting when it comes to the application, either in reference to our own or others' condition. Often we are so taken up with poring over some temporal conditional promise of comfort or deliverance (which we mistake for absolute) that we are ready to conclude ourselves or others to be none of God's children because such a promise is not fulfilled to us or not in our time. This may be a second cause of men's stumbling at the afflictions of the godly.

Stumbling may also proceed from the fact that good men, with an eye of sense, pore over the sufferings of the godly, but do not, with an eye of faith, look either at the gracious promises annexed to them or the blessed issue with which they are attended. Observe that expression of the apostle in 2 Corinthians 4:17, 18: 'For our light affliction, which is but for a moment . . . While we look not at the things which are seen, but at the things which are not seen.' That which makes the godly account their own or their brethren's sufferings light, momentary and inconsiderable is that they look at the things which are not seen. But while men pore over their sufferings, it is no wonder if they are stumbled and take offence. Now this is too common. The best are immersed in sense, and are incomparably more affected with things which are the objects of sense than those which are the objects of faith. They look at what the godly suffer; this their senses inform them; but they consider not what they do now, or hereafter shall, enjoy, which is the true work of faith. This occasions stumbling both ways. As for the wicked's prosperity, men look at what they have in the world and thereupon pronounce them happy; but they consider not that their dishes are sauced and their drink spiced with the wrath of God, and that they have their portion in this life, which is nothing but a bellyful of God's hid treasure (*Psa.* 17:14). Here they have their good things and must hereafter be tormented (*Luke* 16). They stand in slippery places and shall be suddenly tumbled into destruction (*Psa.* 73:18). As for the afflictions of the godly, men look on what they suffer and accordingly judge them miserable, but they consider not how often they are pronounced blessed who suffer for righteousness' sake, or what precious promises are made to them, what reviving cordials are laid in, or what a crown of glory is laid up for them. This is that which makes many people mistake and misjudge. We consider Job's afflictions, but not the end of the Lord. We are apt to look on the dark side of a Christian and to take notice how he is scorched with the sun of afflictions, but do not observe his inward comeliness. His sufferings are in the eye of our sense, but the present promises made to him or the future recompenses laid up for him are not in the eye of our faith, and this causes sad stumbling.

These may suffice as reasons of the truth. I now proceed to application which (omitting many other inferences) shall be only this: to caution you against this miscarriage.

APPLICATION

That which is David's petition to God here, I shall make mine to you. What he desires of God for the godly in reference to his sufferings, I shall desire of you all in reference to my own and my brethren's sufferings at this day. The sum of my caution, counsel, or request is that all of you, whether friends or enemies to us, will take heed you be not offended in us or any way stumble at our sufferings. I am bold to go a little beyond the limits of the text, for whereas it only speaks of their stumbling that are truly godly, and that only by being ashamed and confounded, I extend my caution to all, both godly and wicked (for if the godly, much more the wicked, are apt to stumble, and therefore need cautioning) and to all ways of stumbling and taking offence, so as thereby to offend God. Let none, therefore, upon the account of our sufferings, stumble either at our persons, by disowning or misjudging us; or at our way, by thinking worse of it, or turning from it; or at any weakness you may possibly discover in us, so as thereby to be discouraged and fall from your own steadfastness. These things I might resume and prosecute, but I shall rather direct my caution to such as are enemies and then to such as are friends; to the wicked and then to the godly, that I may (if the Lord please) remove those stumblingblocks at which both the one and the other are apt to fall and miscarry. But I will first give you an account of the reasons that induce me at this time to give you this caution of counsel.

I am afraid lest, by stumbling at our sufferings, you should lose the benefit of the doctrine we have delivered. It was Paul's fear, lest he should run or had run and laboured in vain. Blame us not if we fear the like. 'Tis true indeed, if we have been sincere, our labour cannot be lost as to ourselves. We have delivered our own souls, our work is with the Lord, and our reward with our God. We are to receive our reward not according to our success, but according to our sincerity. But our fear, beloved, is as to you, lest you should have received the grace of God in vain. Should you now stumble and take offence at our sufferings, it might undo what has been done in and upon you by our labours. Were there no more in it but our suffering in our names or reputation with you, I think I should have either wholly omitted, or but lightly touched upon, this matter; but the danger is yours, you may lose as to your souls. Prejudice against your persons, upon the account of our sufferings, may be prejudicial to the effect that the doctrine we have delivered might have upon your hearts.

Again, I am afraid lest religion and the cause of God suffer. As to our persons, 'tis a small matter what you or others say of us. 'Tis a small thing to be judged of you or of man's judgment. Count us what you please, let us be as reprobates, only we would not that the cause of God should suffer and that religion should be wounded. Our fear is that you may stumble in or turn from the way that we have endeavoured to lead you in. If you stand fast in the faith and persevere in practical piety, then though we be offered up upon the sacrifice and service of your faith, we shall joy and rejoice with you all; but if you stumble at our sufferings, as to dislike holiness, to disesteem the sweet and good ways of God, it will be a bitter ingredient in our cup.

I am also afraid lest you should lose the benefit of our sufferings. Beloved, it is not for our own sakes only that we suffer; it is for your benefit, that you may be comforted and confirmed. Read 2 Corinthians 1:6: 'Whether we be afflicted, it is for your consolation and salvation, which is effectual in the enduring of the same sufferings which we also suffer.' Should you take offence and be discouraged, or otherwise stumbled at our afflictions, you would lose that advantage you might otherwise get by them. Yea, that which might be to your benefit would then become your bane and ruin. Upon these and the like inducements, let me press the caution upon you all.

Such of you as are already prejudiced against our persons and ministry, who have stood at a distance and would not come in nor comply with our endeavours for your good, I beseech you, let not our sufferings heighten your prejudice or give you occasion to charge, censure, or condemn us. I see various things at which you will be likely to stumble in this way; give me leave to remove some of them.

You will be ready to say (nay, it is already said by some) that we are justly buffeted for our faults, that it is nothing but what we deserve, as having been busy, censorious, and pragmatical fellows, making divisions and separations amongst our people, taking upon us power to suspend you from the Lord's table, admitting and excluding whom we pleased, exercising a power more arbitrary than ever the bishops did—this is a prejudice deeply rooted in the hearts of many. To which I say, we will in part own the charge. We will not justify ourselves before the Lord, but will say as Nehemiah, 'Thou art just in all that is brought upon us; for thou hast done right, but we have done wickedly' (*Neh.* 9:33). There is sin enough in us to provoke the Lord thus to deal with us.

Yet we have cause to bless the Lord that you have no worse things to lay to our charge, that you cannot write drunkards, loose, debauched, unclean profligate persons upon our doors when we are gone. I hope we shall not, in the thoughts of those who are most prejudiced against us, suffer as thieves, murderers, evildoers, nor unjustly be charged as busybodies in other men's matters. It will not, I hope, be looked upon as presumption, if we take up Samuel's apology. 'Behold, here I am: witness against me before the LORD . . . whose ox have I taken? or whose ass have I taken? or whom have I defrauded?' (*1 Sam.* 12:3). Or Paul's apology: 'I have coveted no man's silver, or gold, or apparel' (*Acts* 20:33). 'We have wronged no man, we have corrupted no man, we have defrauded no man' (2 *Cor.* 7:2). We have not been rigid exactors of that which was our own, much less required that which was not our own, as our and, I hope, your consciences will bear us witness.

As to that which the generality of our people have taken most offence at, *viz.*, our strictness about the sacrament, have we done more than our commission warrants us? Have we not often told you the danger, that to eat and drink unworthily is to eat and drink your own damnation? Can you blame us if we have at once consulted your and our own safety? Will you quarrel or censure us because we would not give you that which, in the state you were, would have been to you a cup of poison, and would certainly have aggravated your damnation? Forgive us this wrong. But who hindered or deprived you of that ordinance ? Was it not your own fault? Have you not been exhorted and entreated to come to us, that you might be instructed and fitted for that ordinance? Yea, if you thought it too much to come to us, have we not offered upon the least invitation to come to you for that purpose? Know you not that the priest's lips should preserve knowledge and that you should seek the law at his mouth? (*Mal.* 2:7). Yet we have sought you and entreated that you would not refuse instruction, but with many of you we have prevailed nothing. Nay, have we not often urged you with this consideration, that your absenting yourselves upon the account of your ignorance would be no excuse? that, as it is a great sin to come without preparation, so it is to refuse those helps by which you might be prepared to come? You have been told that it was the duty of everyone professing Christianity to commemorate the death of Christ in that ordinance; and that it was an undervaluing and a high contempt of Christ and his benefits wilfully to withdraw; that in the sight of God your willingness to come in your ignorance and profaneness, and your refusing to come because you might not come in that state, was as if you had so come. You have been told that God looked upon you as profaners of his ordinance, because you would have done it if you might; so that I hope you will have no just cause to blame us in this particular. What other motive, I pray you, can be rationally imagined as inducing us to show this severity, but fear of sinning against God and of wronging your and our own souls? Had we not been convinced of our duty and the danger of neglecting it, we could have been content to have purchased your favour by a general admission. As for other crimes charged upon us, as preaching sedition, intermeddling with state affairs, *etc.*, I shall only entreat that you would review our sermons, consider our course of preaching (which for the most part has been upon the points of the catechism) and see if there be any just cause to fasten such a charge upon us.

But it will be said that if we do not suffer for our former faults, yet it is for our present fault that we suffer. We may, if we please, submit and continue in our places; it is our wilfulness and obstinacy, fear of losing credit, adherence to a party, *etc.*, that exposes us to suffering. To this I must not make a full answer, nor shall I reflect upon what is done by authority. I acknowledge it my duty to obey passively, and suffer patiently, where I cannot with a good conscience yield active obedience.

I beseech you seriously to consider whether it is probable that a man out of mere obstinacy, or the like principle, will expose himself to such hardships as we are likely to undergo. Which of you would do it?

Make it but your own case, and you will soon discern the unreasonableness of this charge. Consider but what obligations are upon us to continue in our places and ministry, and then see how harsh this unjust censure is.

We are conscious of our duty to God and to the souls of our people. There is a religious tie upon us which nothing in the world but the avoiding of sin can free us from. Beloved, think not that I or my brethren make it a light matter to lay down the exercise of our ministry (I say the exercise; for as to the office itself, none on earth can deprive us of it). I know that word of the apostle, 'Necessity is laid upon me; yea, woe is unto me, if I preach not the gospel' (*1 Cor.* 9:16). I remember that saying of our Saviour, 'No man, having put his hand to the plough, and looking back, is fit for the kingdom of God' (*Luke* 9:62). It is not the heaviest burden (were it a burden only, not a sin) nor the greatest inconveniences that would drive me from my station. I well remember when I entered into this sacred function, I promised not to lay it down till I should lay down the tabernacle of this body; and I desire to look upon it as a high dignity which the Lord has conferred upon me, had I been but a doorkeeper in the house of God (*Psa.* 84:10). But as to my obligation, you see how sacred and inviolable it is. Now, my brethren, you must needs conclude him to have little conscience or sense of duty left upon his spirit, who can out of mere humour and wilfulness shake off such an obligation. And this, beloved, is my hope and confidence, as to myself and many of my brethren, that, should we out of a surly humour (or the like principle) out-run our embassy, our own consciences would raise a storm as effectual to reduce us, as that which brought back Jonah to Nineveh when he fled to Tarshish. Conscience of duty would, I hope, soon drive out obstinacy and frowardness.

But suppose this obligation could be shaken off, there is yet a civil tie, which one would think might be sufficient to hold us, and that is, provision for ourselves and our families. Can it be imagined that a man would, out of mere wilfulness, expose himself and his family to poverty and beggary, maybe to imprisonment or exile? If one or two should be so desperately obstinate, yet that so many hundreds (yea, if reports be true, some thousands) should do it, is a thing attended with the highest improbability, and those such (at least some of them) as for abilities, piety, prudence, and other moral and religious accomplishments, are not inferior to any in the nation. Surely such a censure must needs argue superlative uncharitableness in those that pass it. You cannot judge us to do what we do on mere humour and wilfulness, but you must conclude us to have put off all sense of duty to God and your souls, all humanity and care of ourselves and families, and in that respect to be worse than infidels—in a word, to be sons of Belial, men of most wretched and profligate principles and practices—which if you do, remember that with what judgment you judge others, you yourselves must be judged of God.

But give me leave to put you in mind that the things for which we suffer are of that nature which ordinary

Christians are little able to judge of, and therefore they should not rashly judge us for them. Some of them are such as I must not mention; nor shall I trouble you with many things. For instance, the business of re-ordination, or taking a new ordination at the hands of a bishop. How can I, who have exercised the office of a minister for these fourteen years or upwards, now take a new ordination in a way (to say no more of it) that supposes me no minister till then without notorious dissembling both with God and man? Should one of yourselves among whom I have exercised, urge on me this dilemma: 'If you were no minister before, why did you exercise that function? Why did you preach, pray, and administer sacraments as a public officer in the church? How can you justify the baptizing of our children and administering to us the Lord's supper? If you were indeed a minister, why do you now seek a new commission? Is your old commission expired?'—I seriously profess, beloved, should I submit in this particular, my mouth would be stopped; I should have nothing to say against such an argument. If you say there is no hurt in it, I answer, in my apprehension, it is a taking the name of God in vain, a perverting of an ordinance from its right end, and so in effect making it no ordinance. Besides that, it is a tacit condemning of the ministers of the Reformed churches as no ministers because they lack Episcopal ordination; and (which is not the least mischief) it gives, or may give, just occasion to our people to question the validity of all our ministerial actings. And will you say this is no hurt?

Another instance is the business of the ceremonies. We are not the first to have scruples about them; they have been a bone of contention ever since the beginning of the Reformation, and I fear are likely to continue to be while they are thus pressed. The question is not whether men may impose the wearing of a white garment, the making a cross upon a child's forehead, *etc.*, but whether men may introduce into God's worship and impose upon others such things as are confessedly of human invention, annexing them to or mixing them with God's worship as being significant of inward graces, as tending to edification, and as fitted to excite the dull mind of man or engage him to his duty. Under this consideration and for these ends they are imposed, as the Preface to the *Common Prayer Book* tells you. Meanwhile it is acknowledged that neither Christ nor his apostles used or urged these things; yet we must be imposed upon, and sworn to use and approve them. I appeal to any rational unprejudiced Christian whether there be not enough in this case to beget a conscientious doubting or refusal. Will you say they are not forbidden? No more are thousands of popish superstitions, which yet, I hope, our imposers will not approve of. But I must tell you that to mine and my brethren's apprehensions they are forbidden in those general prohibitions written in Deuteronomy 12:32, Proverbs 30: 6, and Colossians 2:18. Surely he that adds to the worship adds by consequence to the Word of God. If you say, What hurt is in them? I ask, Have they not a tendency to draw men off the spiritual part of God's worship to rest in formalities?

Do they not bring us into more bondage than the Jewish Church, since they had a sacred number of ceremonies and those of God's own appointment; but we, as to the nature and number of ours, are at men's arbitrary judgment and must not cease obeying till they cease imposing? Do they not prove a sad stumblingblock to the more tender, conscientious Christians? And, to add no more, they must needs do hurt in that they do no good. I fear not to say that whatsoever does not do good (I speak of men's inventions) must needs be prejudicial and corrupting to God's worship. I hope then you will forbear to throw after us those rash and harsh censures, as if we wilfully ran ourselves into sufferings. I think it a truth worth our bearing witness to by the greatest sufferings that men ought not to impose nor ought we to submit to human inventions in God's worship when introduced upon pretence of edification or of engaging men to their duty, since such things would reflect upon the wisdom of God, as if he had not known how to make his own ordinance effectual. But I forbear; other instances I might give, but I hasten to what remains.

Another thing which may be an occasion of stumbling and sinning to the profane is that they will rejoice at our sufferings because we have sometimes been troublers of their consciences. They look upon us as pestilent fellows, movers of soul-sedition. They could not swear or drink or oppress others, but the pulpit must ring of it. They hate us because we never prophesied good concerning them; and now they are glad not only to be rid of us, but to see us suffer.

But let me tell you, it is no good argument for Christianity to rejoice in the sufferings of any, though your worst enemies. The command is, 'Rejoice with them that do rejoice, and weep with them that weep' (*Rom.* 12:15). 'Remember them that are in bonds, as bound with them' (*Heb.* 13:3). How contrary is your spirit and practice to these and the like precepts. As for our troubling you, we did it in faithfulness to your souls. And as for our present troubles, suppose it were upon the account of an erroneous conscience (which is the worst that can rationally be supposed of us), yet so long as it is upon the account of conscience, methinks it calls for your pity and compassion.

Let me tell you that there is no such cause of rejoicing as you imagine. If you sin more quietly when we are silenced, conscience will speak at last, the flames of hell will awaken it, and then you will wish that you had both enjoyed and improved your faithful monitors, who out of love to your souls durst not but speak against your sins. Besides, our sufferings presage you no good. If judgment begin at the house of God, the cup may pass from us to you. When God gives order to begin at his sanctuary, he intends utter desolation. In Ezekiel 12:3, 4 the prophet is commanded to remove his stuff, as one going into captivity, as a type to the people. You will see us ere long removing our stuff; what if this be a type to you? Sure I am it is a warning. Let our sufferings be supposed never so just and righteous, yet are there not among you, even among you, sins as heinous and provoking? Do you not fear God, since you are in the same condemnation? Alas, poor fools! were you sensible, it would be small joy to you to have your ministers driven into corners.

I am now to turn my speech to those of you whom the text directly concerns, who look upon our removal as a judgment, and who are burdened for the reproach of our solemn assemblies. There is danger of your stumbling, as the text intimates, and therefore let me caution you also. Take heed you be not offended by, or stumble at, our sufferings. There are many ways you may miscarry. It may possibly be a difficulty with you, how to reconcile our sufferings in this case with God's justice; but remember with the prophet Jeremiah to hold the conclusion however things go (*Jer.* 12:1). You may also meet with temptations to call in question the truth of that doctrine we have delivered to you, or to doubt whether we have taught you the good and the right way; but that which is most common and against which you need to be most cautioned is lest your hands be weakened and your hearts discouraged in the profession of the truth; lest, the shepherds being smitten, the sheep be scattered; lest, by our sufferings, you be moved from the hope of the gospel.

To prevent such miscarriages, consider that our sufferings are not to weaken or discourage but to confirm and encourage you. You quite pervert the reason for our afflictions if you draw arguments of discouragement from them. 'Whether we be afflicted, it is for your consolation' (2 *Cor.* 1:6). We are put to lead that you may the more cheerfully follow, if called to it. 'Many of the brethren in the Lord [wax] confident by my bonds' (*Phil.* 1:14). That was indeed a right improvement of Paul's sufferings. I mean, not that you should run yourselves upon sufferings or do anything unlawful or unwarrantable to pull afflictions upon your own heads. The serpent's wisdom is commendable when in conjunction with the dove's simplicity and innocency; but if the cup (which ordinarily goes round) be put into your hands, our example should be your encouragement to drink it more cheerfully. As for doing anything (or so much as speaking) against civil authority upon our account, far be it from us to urge you to it. Nay, we charge you to keep the way of duty and loyalty to sovereign authority. 'The wrath of man worketh not the righteousness of God' (*James* 1:20). But if you are called out to bear witness (as we conceive we now are) to the truth of God and the purity of his worship and ordinances, then we say to you, look on us and do likewise. Choose rather to suffer than sin. We have preached the truth, and we now are called to seal it with the loss of our livelihood and liberty in some measure. Let not our sufferings weaken or unsettle, but rather strengthen your faith and heighten your resolution: our afflictions should be your encouragements.

Nor should the bitter scoffs and reproaches that you may undergo for our sakes at all move you. I doubt not you will have the scorn as well as the loss. It will be said to you in a way of derision, as the sons of the prophet said to Elisha, 'Knowest thou that the LORD will take away thy master from thy head to day?' (*2 Kings* 2:3). So, know you not that your beloved minister is going?

As they said to David, 'Where is thy God?' (*Psa.* 42:10), so to you, 'Where is your minister, whom you almost made a god of?' This will be a sword in your bones. Such reproaches, added to your loss, will be ready to break the heart of those who prize their faithful ministers, as they ought to do; to whom they are (as Chrysostom to his people) equally necessary as the sun in the firmament. But it is your part to arm yourselves with courage and patience, and to observe that double rule of Solomon in Proverbs 26:4, 5, 'Answer not a fool according to his folly, lest thou also be like unto him,'—that is, do not render reproach for reproach, or railing for railing, nor yet be deprived of your patience or constancy, which is his design. Yet 'answer a fool according to his folly, lest he be wise in his own conceit'—that is, chide and rebuke him; let him know that he has no true cause of rejoicing in the loss of a faithful ministry, and that he shall one day know the worth of that mercy that now he disregards and undervalues.

Though it must be acknowledged as one of God's saddest dispensations to take away a faithful ministry and to send a famine of the Word, yet this must not discourage us so as to make us desist from holiness. Bless God that you ever had such a mercy and got good by it. Bewail the sin that has deprived you of it; but take heed you do not upon this account turn aside, as Joash when good Jehoiada was dead, and as the Israelites when Moses was gone. Rather call to mind what we have spoken for your confirmation. Give diligence when we are gone to have the things in remembrance that you have heard from us. And as an encouraging word (with which I shall conclude) assure yourselves that even this sad providence is within the compass of those things in the promise, 'All things work together for good to them that love God' (*Rom.* 8:28). The loss of a faithful minister may be sanctified to effect that good in and for you, which the enjoyment of him has not done. You mistake if you think we have done preaching; no, we are only called to preach to you out of the pulpit of the cross; and I hope it may be said of us, as of Abel, though we are dead we yet speak (*Heb.* 11:4). And why may it not be hoped that our preaching out of that pulpit may be more effectual than out of this? That is a comfortable word to those that can apply it, 1 Corinthians 3:22—'Whether Paul, or Apollos, or Cephas, or the world, or life, or death, or things present, or things to come; all are yours,' *i.e.*, they are ordained for your benefit. All God's disposals of us (whatever you may think) are for your advantage; and through grace I shall, in confidence thereof, say with the apostle, 'If I be offered upon the sacrifice and service of your faith, I joy, and rejoice with you all' (*Phil.* 2:17). If my sufferings attain their end, which is your consolation and salvation, I shall through grace bless God in making use of me to that purpose. In the meanwhile, that is a staying word to my soul (*Luke* 13:33), 'It cannot be that a prophet perish out of Jerusalem,' that is, be taken away before he has done his work. I know God is not tied to one way; he can make our silence speak louder and more effectually than all our sermons have done.

To conclude then, let me repeat my request to you all. Let none of you stumble or take offence at our sufferings. Let me humbly use the words of our blessed Saviour, 'Blessed is he, whosoever shall not be offended in me' (*Matt.* 11:6). Let not our enemies rejoice or censure us, let not our friends sorrow as without hope, but let all wait and observe the issue, and I doubt not but God in his own time will manifest to the world, that his intentions (even in this thing) were good towards his faithful ministers and waiting people. This shall be as a refiner's fire, and as fuller's soap, to purify the sons of Levi. This shall be the fruit, even the taking away of Jacob's sin (*Isa.* 27:9). 'The LORD will not cast off his people, neither will he forsake his inheritance. But judgment shall return unto righteousness: and all the upright in heart shall follow it' (*Psa.* 94:14, 15).

As for the third doctrine, that a gracious soul fears and prays against the evil influence that his sufferings might have upon others, I shall, as God enables, put it into practice on your behalf, and shall take up the psalmist's words: 'Let not them that wait on thee, O Lord GOD of hosts, be ashamed for my sake: let not those that seek thee be confounded for my sake, O God of Israel.'

JOHN WHITLOCK

LIFE

The son of a London merchant, John Whitlock was born in 1625. He studied at Emmanuel College, where his tutor was Ralph Cudworth, the leader of the 'Cambridge Platonists,' and graduated B.A. in 1645 and M.A. in 1649. At Cambridge a remarkable friendship began with William Reynolds; they lived together under the same roof for fifty years, and it was said that the two seemed to have but one soul. When in 1645 Whitlock commenced his ministry at Leighton Buzzard, he was joined by Reynolds. Three years later, being invited to Aylesbury, he agreed to share the two places (Aylesbury and Leighton) with the friend. He was deprived of his maintenance in 1649 for refusing the Engagement, but in 1651 the Marquis of Dorchester presented him to the vicarage of St Mary's, Nottingham; here Reynolds joined him as lecturer. Later in the same year, they were both ordained by the classis in London and, on their return, established a Presbyterian discipline in the church at Nottingham.

In July 1662 Whitlock was indicted for not reading the common prayer and, although the Act of Uniformity was not yet in force, he was suspended and his church sequestered. Consequently his farewell sermons were delivered at his Friday lecture on 27 June and 6 July. He was forced to leave Nottingham and preached in various places in the Midlands, settling at Mansfield in 1668. He was imprisoned at Nottingham in 1685 and moved, still in confinement, to Hull later in the same year. As a result of the Indulgence in 1687, he was able to return to Nottingham and resume his ministry, a meeting-house being erected for the purpose in 1690-1. Whitlock's close association with Reynolds was ended by the latter's death in 1698, but he himself lived on to the age of 83. After his death in 1708, his son succeeded him in the ministry at Nottingham. Apart from single sermons, Whitlock's chief published works were *A Short Account of the Life of Rev. William Reynolds* and *The Great Duty and Comfortable Evidence*.

REMEMBER, HOLD FAST AND REPENT

Remember therefore how thou hast received and heard, and hold fast, and repent.
Revelation 3:3

Beloved, when I entered on this verse in the course of my Friday lecture, I little thought that I had so short a time to preach among you. I hoped I should have enjoyed some further opportunities for some few weeks, at least as long as the Act of Uniformity allows. But it has pleased God by his wise and holy providence to order it otherwise, I being suspended from preaching here from this day forward, for nonconformity. How far rightly or legally on man's part, I shall not dispute, but leave to the righteous God to determine. I desire that both you and I may not eye man but God in this dispensation. I did not think to have preached my farewell sermon to you from these words, but having begun this text and finding the matter of it so seasonable and suitable to this sad occasion, I shall by God's assistance proceed in the handling of it.

Since it is probable that I shall preach no more to you, I judge it very seasonable to leave the exhortation in the text with you, to call upon you to remember what and how you have received and heard, and to hold fast those wholesome truths you have heard, and those precious ordinances (at least the remembrance, impressions, and gracious effects of them) that you have enjoyed and been privileged with. Also, to repent of those sins, which have provoked and may further provoke God to come on us as a thief, to take away many of his ministers from among us.

The words, as I have already shown, are Christ's counsel to a languishing church and to decayed Christians to repair decayed godliness and religion in a church and in the hearts and lives of particular Christians. This renders them more seasonable to these days we live in and to the condition of many of our souls. I have already opened the doctrine and confirmed it by several scriptures, namely, that it is the duty both of churches and particular Christians—and a special means to recover them from formality, decays and deadness in religion and the exercise of grace—to remember what and how they have received and heard. I should now proceed to give you the reasons of the doctrine, but I shall choose rather to reserve them to the application, and then press them as motives to enforce the counsel and exhortation grounded on the text and doctrine; and so I shall immediately proceed to the application.

The first use of the doctrine is one of *information*. It informs us that there is somewhat more required of

Christians than bare hearing of sermons, receiving and partaking of sacraments and other ordinances. It is not enough to hear and receive, but it is the duty of Christians also to remember what and how they have received and heard, what good they have got by, and what communion with God they have enjoyed in the use of the Word and ordinances.

The doctrine also informs us what it is we are to make the rule of our faith and practice, namely, the Word of God contained in the Scriptures and the truths you have heard rightly grounded thereon. They ought to be the standard to which we should bring all doctrines preached, all things introduced into divine worship and imposed upon us in practice. Bring all things to this test. It is your duty to search and study the Scriptures and bring all things to the law and to the testimony. If they speak not according to these, it is because there is no light in them. You must not believe every spirit, but try the spirits whether they be of God. When either doctrine or worship is corrupted in a church, the way to reform both is not to fly to human authority or antiquity, but to the golden rule of the Word. This is the only safe rule. Other rules may err, but this is infallible.

The second use of the doctrine is one of *reproof*. It reproves forgetful hearers, such as seem very eager in hearing and receiving divine truths and attending on gospel ordinances, but are not careful to remember what and how they have received and heard. It reproves such as return not to the things they have heard, but leave all behind them; such (as a divine expresses it) who come from duties as from a grave, where they leave their dearest friends behind them, not as from a distribution from which they carry something with them. Of such hearers as these the Apostle James speaks (*James* 1:22-24). I speak not here of the forgetfulness that proceeds merely from weakness, that is bewailed and is the burden of their souls. This is indeed an infirmity to be bewailed, yet deserves pity and compassion from men rather than reproof. The forgetfulness this text reproves is that which proceeds from carelessness, when men do not make conscience of the duty pressed in the text, namely, remembering how they have received and heard.

The third and last use of this text which I shall further make and insist on is one of *exhortation*. It exhorts all of you to the practice of the duty in the text. Oh, labour to remember what and how you have received and heard. I am likely no more to speak to you publicly in the name of the Lord. Let me therefore leave this counsel and exhortation with you as that which may be of great use to you in hours of temptation that may come upon you. I beseech you, beloved, by the mercies of God, in the bowels of Christ, and out of the respect you bear to your own precious and immortal souls, that you would labour and endeavour to remember those soul-saving truths and precious ordinances you have received, heard and enjoyed, and those impressions you have felt upon your hearts from them. Oh, be not forgetful hearers! Let not the truths of God slip out of your minds.

Beloved, I may say to you, there is scarce any truth necessary to salvation but you have heard of it once and again from some or other of God's messengers that have been sent to you, though not without the mixtures of sin and weakness as to the instruments (which God in mercy pardon). You have heard what God is and how he will be worshipped, even in spirit and in truth, and not according to the inventions and traditions of men. You have heard the doctrine of God's decrees and of his works of creation and providence opened and applied. You have heard of the sinful and miserable condition of a man in a natural condition. You have heard the doctrine of the covenant of grace and of the means of our recovery by Christ alone. You have had Christ set before you in his person, natures, offices, obedience, and sufferings. You have heard many other both theoretical and practical truths set before you in preaching, expounding, and catechizing; and by these you have been antidoted against popish, Socinian, and Arminian errors, and many others. Oh, labour to remember these. Keep them by you as a choice treasure. Lay them up in your heads and hearts, that you may be able to bring out of your treasury things both new and old. Oh, let not any of the truths of God slip out of your minds or be as water spilt upon the ground. Ministers must die, but let not the truths of God die in your hearts. Ministers may be forcibly parted from you and have their mouths stopped, as ours and many others are and are likely to be; yet let not the Word of truth depart out of your minds when we are gone. Let the Word of God, even that Word of his that we have spoken to you in his name, abide with you for ever. Let it live with you, and let it die with you also. Oh, let truth be written on your hearts, as with the point of a diamond, never to be erased. A stony heart is a grievous plague, but an iron memory is a great mercy. Oh, therefore remember what you have heard in point of doctrine, and remember also the counsels and directions you have had given to you, as to the performance of public, family, secret, and relative duties.

Remember the warnings you have had against sin. Sinners, you have been warned against your sins. You drunkard, swearer, sabbath-breaker, unclean person, you enemy to godliness, you scorner and scoffer at and persecutor of religion; yea, you formalists, hypocrites, that rest in civility, morality, or outside performances; you have been warned of the danger of your condition, of the wrath of God hanging over your heads for these sins, of the necessity of repentance for and from your sins and of faith in Christ if ever you would be saved. Remember the forewarnings you have had of God's judgments, of the things you now fear, yea feel. Christians, have you not been told many a time of the judgments that follow wantonness in opinion and practice? and of the judgments that God inflicts upon mere professors of the faith for their deadnesses, worldlinesses, decays and carnal policies? And you that are saints, remember what soul-refreshing comforts you have had in and from the Word of God. Remember how plainly, purely, powerfully, plentifully the Word of God has been preached and ordinances dispensed among you. And remember also with what seriousness of spirit, high estimation, holy affection, readiness of mind, strong resolution, powerful impressions you have heard and received the Word and ordinances of God, and what gracious effects you have found from them.

Now to press this exhortation, I shall first lay down some motives to stir you up to this duty of remembering how you have received and heard. The first is this. The truths you have heard and ordinances you have partaken of were not of use only for the time past or present, while you were or are hearing or receiving them, but they are of use a great while after. The sermons you have long since heard and sacraments you have received may do your souls good as long as you live. The virtue and use of the Word and ordinances may and does often put forth itself long after the participation of them; and therefore you should remember them that you may bring them forth for use in the time to come, which you cannot do if you let them slip out of your heads and hearts. The truths of God are as treasuries and storehouses, which are not only for present use, but for time to come, for men to live on a great while after, in times of want and scarcity. And know this, Christians, you may have occasion to make use of every truth you have heard, before you die sooner or later, even those which, while you hear them, may seem to be of little use. To a man in prosperity the doctrine of suffering and affliction may not seem so seasonable, or to one in adversity to press the duties of one in a prosperous state; but yet these may come to be of great advantage to you. The sermons you have heard many years since and that you hear this day may prove food to your souls many years hence. 'Who among you will give ear to this? who will hearken and hear for the time to come?' (*Isa.* 42:23). Oh, Christians, do labour to be such hearers.

Remember how you have received. Remember old truths, former sermons, Sabbaths, sacraments; for the time may come, and you know not how soon, when you may have little else to live upon but the old store, even what you have formerly received and heard. You may be cut short in your spiritual opportunities, you may have few, at least comparatively, of those helps you have enjoyed, or enjoy ordinances in such a way as may not yield satisfaction to your consciences; and then the remembrance of what you have received and what communion with God you have enjoyed will be very precious. Times may come—bear with the expression—when you may have little but cold dishes to feed upon. In a time of scarcity, when there is little corn to be reaped, it is some comfort to have some in the barn or storehouse. The corn Joseph laid up in years of plenty helped to preserve himself and his whole family and all the land of Egypt. And, if you are careful to remember how you have received and heard, you may be able to feed yourselves and others in a time of scarcity of spiritual opportunities, if for your and others' sins God should bring it on you. Let me therefore leave the counsel in the text with you: go to the old store. Feed on cold meat, when you lack warm. Warm it again on your hearts by meditation and a practical remembrance of the Word. Those things that, when you had full meals and full stomachs, you lightly esteemed, when your souls are hungry and when soul-provision is scarce, you may find and taste much sweetness in them.

A third motive to excite you to remember how you have received and heard is this. Consider that God remembers how you have received and heard, and he will make you remember it also and call you to an account for the things you have received and heard. He remembers all the truths that have been delivered to you, the warnings you have had, the sermons you have heard, the sacraments you have received, and all other means of grace you have enjoyed. Though you forget them, he remembers how plainly, purely, plentifully, and with what affection you have received them. And consider further, God will call you to account for all these things, what good you have got by them, what improvement you have made of them, whether you have been brought to repentance and faith by them, and what progress in faith and holiness you, who profess yourselves to be saints, have made under them. Oh, therefore, seeing God remembers these, do you also remember them.

A fourth motive to excite you to this duty of remembering how you have received and heard is this. Consider the great benefit and usefulness of this remembrance; it will be of very great use and advantage to your souls. This I shall somewhat largely insist on. And the particulars I shall hint under this head may serve not only as motives to excite you to the practice of this duty, but also as directions, to direct you what use you should make of the truths and ordinances you have formerly received.

The first benefit of remembering how you have received and heard is that it will, by the blessing of God upon it, prove a choice antidote against errors in doctrine and also against corruption in the worship of God, if ever any of these come to be vented among you or obtruded and imposed upon you. If doctrines come to be preached that tend to the beating down of the power of godliness and the practice of holiness, or that are opposed to the free grace of God in election or justification (crying up conditional decrees upon a foresight of faith, or works, or perseverance, or introducing man's works in the business of justification); or if men preach such doctrines as advance the power of nature, the freedom of man's will, or if they teach that true believers may finally and totally fall from grace—the remembrance of what you have received and heard, with the experience of the work of God in your own hearts (you who are saints), will preserve you from such errors, and help you to confute these and such like false doctrines, and teach you to say, 'We have not so learned Christ.' The reason why men slide into new errors or old ones newly patched up is because they let slip old truths. If you forget truths you have heard, you lose your touchstone to try doctrines by, and then you may be easily cheated with counterfeit metal instead of gold. You will be like a ship that has lost its anchor or compass; you will go you know not whither and be in danger of splitting upon the rocks. And this will also safeguard you against human inventions, mingled with and obtruded on men in the worship of God. You will be able to tell their authors that you have so learned to worship God; and it will teach you to reason, Did Christ or his apostles appoint ordinances to be thus or thus dispensed? Labour therefore to remember, and make this use of your remembrance how you have received and heard.

A second benefit of remembering how you have received and heard is this. It will be, by God's blessing, a notable means to shame and humble you for all your uneven and unworthy application of those savoury truths and precious ordinances you have been partakers of. It will make you ashamed of your deadness, dullness, formality in duties, and declinings and decays in grace. And you should endeavour thus to improve your remembrance of former receipts of mercy. It will make you say to your souls, Has my conduct been in keeping with divine truth? Have I followed the directions and taken the warnings God has given me? Oh, what a vile, sinful wretch have I been! How came I to walk so out of step with the grace of God in the gospel? It will make you blush when you remember how plainly, purely, powerfully and plentifully the ordinances have been dispensed to you. It will cause you to lament that you have had so impure a heart and life under such pure ordinances; that there has been no more of the power of godliness expressed in your conduct when you have lived under such powerful ministries; that you have brought forth so little fruit; that you have been and are no more fat and flourishing in the courts of God under that plenty of heavenly manna that has been rained down upon you, and those soul-fattening ordinances you have partaken of! Thus improve your remembrance how you have received and heard. When you find your hearts growing dead and cold, Oh, then say, Was it wont to be thus? Where are those high estimations, those lively affections, those holy resolutions, that seriousness of spirit, those powerful impressions and gracious effects of the Word and sacraments that I once found in and under them? Oh, let this consideration excite you to this duty in the text, and make the benefit of former gospel-enjoyments, and the good you found in them to shame and humble you that you have made no better use of them.

A third benefit of remembering how you have received and heard is that, through the blessing of God upon it, it will be a means and help to keep from sin in practice. It will be a special preservative against the infection of the sins of the days and times into which you may be cast. As you desire to be preserved from sin, make conscience of this duty; and it will be a means to restore you again when you have fallen into sin. See Psalm 119:9, 11—hiding the Word of God in his heart was a means of keeping David from sinning against God. Attending to the Word of God is prescribed by him as a means to cleanse the ways even of a young man. This will keep you from being superstitious, profane and loose when others are so; but if once you forget what and how you have received, you will soon swim down the stream with others and quickly be overrun with sin. Peter first forgot the word of warning Christ had given him, and then he soon forgot himself and his own duty and fell into that foul sin of denying his Lord and Master. Oh, therefore remember how you have received and heard, and improve your remembrance of it to preserve you from falling into sin and to recover you when you are fallen. When you are tempted to sin, say, I have been otherwise taught; I have not so learned Christ; I have been warned against such and such sins. As Peter's forgetfulness of Christ's words was the cause of his fall, so it was the remembrance of what Christ had spoken that helped to raise him up again, when he was fallen. And you should endeavour to improve the remembrance of the words of Christ unto this end.

A fourth benefit of the remembrance of how you have received and heard is that it will be a spur to quicken you to duty and a means to excite and strengthen grace (see 2 *Tim.* 1:6, 2 *Pet.* 1:12-15; 3:1, 2). In all these places you will find that this remembrance of what men have received and heard is a means to stir up the gifts and graces of God's Spirit in them. When you remember what you have received from God in ordinances and in the performance of holy duties, it will make you desirous to converse in them and to love them the better, as long as ever you live. You will say, It is good to be here; you will never be weary of waiting upon God whilst you retain a savoury remembrance of the sweetness, power and efficacy you have found and felt in the Word and ordinances of God. And this will also be a means to increase and strengthen grace in the soul. Grace in the soul is nourished by the same means by which it is begotten. Those promises that inclined the heart to believe at first will now, being remembered and fed upon by faith, raise faith to higher pitches and degrees. Remembering your former experiences of God's helping you when you have been in straits will help you to trust in God in future straits and trials. Labour therefore to remember and to make this use of the remembrance of what and how you have received and heard, to quicken you to a more constant attendance on God in ordinances and to increase and strengthen grace in your souls.

The remembrance of how you have received and heard will be of great use and advantage to your souls, for it will keep up in your judgments an high estimation of, and in your affections a sincere love to, those precious truths and those plain, pure and powerful dispensations of ordinances you have partaken of, even when by sickness or any other hand of God upon you, you may be deprived of the actual enjoyment of them. If God should remove ministers and ordinances from you or you from them so that you cannot enjoy them as you have done, yet the very remembrance of them will be precious when you remember what heart-warmings you have had under them. Labour to make this remembrance of old truths and former enjoyments a means to make you esteem and love them.

A sixth benefit of remembering how you have received and heard is that it will keep up in you earnest and hungering desires. It will stir up in you a mighty spirit of prayer for the keeping and restoring, when you have lost them, of those precious truths and ordinances in which you have found so much of God. It will cause you to say with the disciples, 'Lord, evermore give us this bread.' It will and should cause you to cry to your Father for the bread of life, to imitate the language of the psalmist as in Psalm 42:1, 2 and Psalm 63:1, 2. David remembered what he had seen of the power and glory of God in the sanctuary, and this set his soul a-longing for the restoring again of those blessed opportunities he had been privileged with. Oh, make this remembrance of how you have received and heard to cause you to wrestle with God in prayer for the continuance and restitution of those comfortable sabbaths and sacraments, that pure and powerful preaching, praying and administration of ordinances, which God has vouchsafed. It was this remembrance of what and how he had received that made that holy martyr, Bishop Latimer, cry out, 'Lord, restore the gospel once again to England.' And in such or the like cases, it should make you, and will make you, pray that God would restore the liberty of his ministers and the power and purity of his ordinances, and try you whether you will not through his grace improve them better than you have done.

A seventh benefit of this remembering how you have received and heard is that it will bring into your souls the comfort and sweetness of former truths and ordinances. It will be as the rolling of a sweet morsel under your tongue. You may hereby reap the benefit of former sermons and sacraments many years hence. Many times truth is more sweet and makes a more powerful impression on the soul in meditation and repetition of it than it did at its first delivery. And so it may do in you, if you are careful in the practice of this duty.

Lastly, the remembering of what and how you have received and heard may and will bear up your hearts under, and fortify them against, all suffering and persecution you may meet with for the sake of Christ, when you remember the warnings Christ has given you (*John* 16:1, 2) and the grounds of comfort you have found in the Word of God. Improve your remembrance of truths for this end.

So much for the motives to stir you up to the practice of this duty in the text. And these last eight particulars may serve also to direct you what use you should make of the remembrance of what and how you have received.

I shall proceed to add some few directions to direct you how and after what manner you should remember what and how you have received.

Remember what and how you have received and heard, *thankfully*. Oh, be thankful, Christians, that you have enjoyed the Word and ordinances of God so long, and that with so much plainness, power, purity and plenty. Though you should never enjoy them again, yet you have cause to bless God that you have enjoyed the Word, sacraments, ministers so long, above not only your desires, but also your expectations. Especially be thankful, you that have received Christ and grace through these. Be thankful that you have received grace before you have lost any of the means of grace, and that Christ and your souls have met, before you and your ministers have parted.

Remember how you have received and heard, *penitentially and sorrowfully*. Be penitent and sorrowful that you prized and improved truths and ordinances no better, got no more good by them, grew no more in grace under them, gained no more power against corruptions, or ability to do and suffer by them while you did enjoy them. And remember sorrowfully how you have received, if you have lost or should lose any of your opportunities. When the ways of Zion mourn, it is sure the sons of Zion should mourn. You should be sorrowful for the solemn assemblies; the reproach of them should be a burden unto Christians. You should remember your gospel-enjoyments with tears, as did those in Psalm 137:1, 2 who wept when they remembered Zion (see also *Psa.* 42:3). Christians in such a case should bewail the loss of ordinances and of so many of God's ministers.

Christians should especially remember gospel mercies penitentially, in the lack of them when they have helped to sin them away by their unfruitful and unworthy walking. Know, Christians, it is the sins of ministers and people that stop the mouths of ministers and deprive a people at any time of any of the tokens of God's presence. You should, in such a case and condition, with sorrow of heart say, We once enjoyed comfortable days of the Son of man, but by our deadness, spiritual wantonness and unfruitfulness we have now sinned them away.

Remember what and how you have received, *affectionately and practically*. It is not a mere notional, but an affectionate and practical remembrance of truths received and ordinances enjoyed that I now press upon you. Remember them with burning and inflamed hearts. Remember truths so as to practise them; to love truth and to live in truth, and ordinances, so as to live up to them, so as to have pure hearts agreeable to pure ordinances, the power of religion in your conduct agreeable to powerful ministries. Remember the Word of truth to direct your practice, even as a compass to sail by in a troublesome sea and a dark night and as a copy to write after. Remember what you have heard so as to set on the practice of duties you have been exhorted to and directed in, and to avoid the sins you have been warned against. So remember as to improve your remembrance of truth to those eight uses, before specified for your comfort and support under sufferings, namely, as an antidote against error in doctrine and corruption in worship, to humble for and keep you from sin, to quicken to duty, to make you prize, love, pray for, and long after the Word.

Having given you some directions how you should remember what and how you have received and heard, I shall now close this doctrine by adding some means and helps to enable you to the performance of the duty I have been exhorting you to.

A first means or help to enable you to remember what you have received and heard is to labour after a sincere love to the Word, ordinances and ministers of Christ. Love truth, and you will the more easily remember it. You will not suddenly or easily forget what you dearly love. Affection is a very great help to memory. Receive truth in your love and affection, and then you will keep it in your minds and memories. A man will remember what his mind and heart is set upon. A special means to keep truth in your heads is to labour that it may be engraven in your hearts. Look upon the Word and ordinances of God as your treasury, and you will then be sure, at least practically, to remember it. Men scarcely forget where they have laid their treasure or their jewels, though they may forget where they have laid things of lesser moment. Love does and will renew and revive the object loved in the mind and in the thoughts. Affection to divine objects is the safest lock and key to secure spiritual treasures. David loved the law, and then he could do no other but make it his meditation all the day long (*Psa.* 119:97).

A second help or means to enable you to remember what and how you have received and heard, is to apply and appropriate truths and ordinances to your own souls. Labour to ensure your interest in Christ, in the covenant of grace, and in the great truths of the gospel; and that will much further your remembering of them. You will be careful to remember what you look on as your chief interests. Though men may forget others' business, they will hardly forget their own, especially if they be matters of great concern, matters in which their whole estate is concerned, or matters of life and death. And such are the things you have received and heard in the gospel. When you hear the Word, say, 'There God spoke to my soul.' Men forget truths because they are apt to put them off to others and not to look on themselves as concerned in them. Oh, therefore look on your soul as concerned in what you have heard and received, and this will help you to remember it.

A third means to help you to remember what you have received and heard is serious and frequent meditation and contemplation on what you have heard. This is a great help to memory. Divine meditation fixes truths in the head and fastens them in the heart. 'Mary kept all these things, and pondered them in her heart' (*Luke* 2:19). Be therefore much in meditation.

A fourth means to further your remembrance of what you have received and heard is holy conference. This Moses directs to in Deuteronomy 6:6-9, as a means to keep the things of God in the heart. This is as the driving home of the nail. That which one forgets another may remember. Improve private conference, and speak often one to another; and, when you meet together, be more spiritual, savoury and profitable in your discourse than heretofore you have been, and especially when you may have fewer public opportunities. Time may come when this may be one of the best helps you have. It may be God will cut you short of many public advantages to chasten you for your not using or improving the private communion of saints and to quicken you to use and improve holy conference and other private duties more and better.

A fifth means to help you to remember what and how you have received and heard is earnest and fervent prayer to God, that he would strengthen your memories and give his Spirit to you according to his promise to bring all things to your remembrance. Commit truths to the Spirit's keeping, and trust not only to your own memories. Often plead that promise with God (*John*

14:26). Christ would not trust his disciples alone with his sermons. He knew their memories were slippery, but he entrusts his Spirit to bring things to their remembrance; and the Spirit can and will bring truths to your remembrance, in the most seasonable time.

Lastly, endeavour to practise the things you have received and heard, and that will be a means to help you to remember them. Labour to get good by the Word and ordinances, and you will not soon forget them. He who daily writes after a copy will be better able to remember it long after. 'I will never forget thy precepts: for with them thou hast quickened me' (*Psa.* 119:93). Those sermons, sacraments and other ordinances, in and by which God has quickened and comforted you, you will not forget.

So much for handling this doctrine. Might I have had liberty to preach to you as long as I hoped and the law allowed, I should have handled the two other directions in the text, 'Hold fast' and 'Repent.' But seeing I am likely to preach to you no more, I shall briefly touch upon them, and leave them with you in a way of exhortation.

The second direction Christ gives to this church in order to recover her from her deadness and formality is to *hold fast* what she had received. The doctrine is this: it is the duty of Christians, and a means to recover declining churches and Christians, to hold fast what they have received and heard. And indeed without this you cannot be strengthened by it. That which you have lost and let slip will do you but little good. You must not only remember, but also hold fast. I shall not handle this doctrinally. Time will not permit it, and besides, I have formerly insisted on this doctrine and duty from the 13th and 25th verses of the second chapter. I shall therefore only leave the exhortation with you. Hold fast what you have received and heard.

And here I shall briefly show you what you should hold fast, against what, and how.

First, what you should hold fast. Hold fast the doctrine of the gospel you have received and heard. Do not let go any truth of God. 'Buy the truth, and sell it not' at any price (*Prov.* 23:23). You may meet with those that would pluck it from you; but be sure you hold it fast (2 *Tim.* 1:13, 14).

Hold fast the plain, pure and powerful ordinances of God. Oh, do not let these go, at least not through your default. Let them not go for want of prayers and tears to keep them.

Be sure you hold fast a high estimation of the Word and pure ordinances of God. If ever you should lack them, yet prize and esteem them as your treasure. Let the lack of spiritual mercies teach you more to value the worth of them. Though you should lose many of your mercies and opportunities, yet be sure you do not lose your esteem of them.

Be sure you hold fast your love to the truths and ordinances of God, as well in the lack, as in the enjoyment of them. Love the Word, and love the ministers of Christ, even when you are deprived of them.

Hold fast your appetite for and stomach to the Word

and ordinances of God. Though you should lose some of your meat, take heed you lose not your stomach with your meat. If you have less food, yet you should labour to have the better stomachs. Oh, beg of God that though he should suffer your food to fail, yet that he would not take away your appetites, but keep them fresh and lively. In temporals it would be a mercy if men who lacked meat lacked a stomach for it; but in spirituals it will be a mercy, though you should have little food, yet to have a good stomach continued. This will be a pledge of God's returning and restoring absent but desired mercies. For God has said that he will satisfy the hungry soul with bread.

Lastly, be sure you hold fast the good you have got by the Word, prayer, sacraments, the ministers and ordinances of Christ. Though you should part with these things themselves, yet be sure you retain and hold fast the good you have got by them, and those impressions of God's Spirit that have been made on your hearts through and under them.

Secondly, all this you must hold fast, against the fraud and deceit of seducers and deceivers, who would go about to cheat and cozen[1] you of the great and precious truths of the gospel, and of the true worship of God. The apostle tells you that men will arise who will privily bring in damnable heresies (2 *Pet.* 2:1-3), and the Apostle Paul speaks of the sleights and cunning craftiness of men and their methods to deceive (*Eph.* 4:14). They will perhaps plead antiquity, tradition, the authority of the

[1] That is, 'beguile', 'dupe'.—P.

Church, the consent of ancient Fathers, custom, example, yea, a seeming reason for many opinions and practices. But, Christians, be not cheated of your religion; but that which you have received of the Lord Christ and has been delivered to you by the apostles of the Word, those truths and instructions of Christ, do you hold fast.

Hold fast the truths and ordinances of Christ against the force and violence of persecutors. As you should not be fawned, so neither should you be frighted out of anyone truth or ordinance of God, or out of your love to, or desire after, or owning of them.

Thirdly, the means to enable you to hold fast what you have received: The first is diligent attendance on the public ordinances and worship of God, if and when you can enjoy them in any measure according to God's will, though not altogether with the kind of administration that you desire. I hope that for the sake of the many praying, believing, hungry souls that are to be found in this place, God may provide you in his due time with such teachers as may give you some wholesome food and not feed you with stones instead of bread. For some such I doubt not will be found, if God shall vouchsafe to you the mercy of a faithful minister. Though I dare not advise you actively to join in anything that is in itself or in your judgment evil, till you be satisfied about it, yet I must advise you to take heed of separation from the church, or from what is good, and God's own ordinance. If sound truth be powerfully preached, make use of and improve that, though you cannot approve everything the minister does. I the rather add this because there are many who, if ministers do but mention the loss of ministers, are ready presently to accuse them of monopolizing all religion to themselves and to their party. But far be this from me and others. I know while the best of men are on earth, there is likely to be variety of apprehensions; and some men of sound judgment in the main and of holy lives may satisfy themselves in the lawfulness of some things that others judge sinful. And if God send such to you, though I do not bid you approve their practice or justify what they do, yet bless God for them and improve their gifts and graces. And yet at the same time you have just cause to bewail the laying aside of so many hundreds of ministers. Had so many hundreds of ministers died a natural death in one day, you would have looked upon it as a great judgment; and surely it is no less when so many die a civil death!

A second means to enable you to hold fast what you have received is to be much in conference, in considering one the other, to provoke to love and to good works (*Heb.* 10:23-25). As this is a help to remembering, so also to holding fast what you have received.

Hold fast the Word and ordinances by prayer that God would continue them and that he would keep them in your minds and hearts.

Be sure you hold fast God and Christ by faith. It is God that vouchsafes all these to you; if the streams should fail, be sure you hold fast the fountain, and you will be well, and you will do well.

The last counsel and direction Christ gives to this languishing church is to *repent*. Whence observe that repentance is a sovereign means to repair decayed religion and godliness in a church and in the souls of men. Repentance is the soul's physic,[1] which purges out ill humours, heals the soul's diseases, and restores it to a healthful constitution.

I intend not to handle this, but to turn it into an exhortation. Let me leave this counsel and exhortation with all of you this day, as that which probably may be the last and I am sure is the best counsel I can give. Oh, repent, repent, both sinners and saints. Repent, thou drunkard, swearer, sabbath-breaker, unclean person, thou opposer of godliness, or whatever else thy sin be. Remember thou hast been called on to repent this day! Oh, repent while it is called today, before the things that belong to your peace be hid from your eyes. Repent even all, both bad and good, of those sins that have brought these judgments upon us, which this day we lie under.

More particularly, repent of that opposition against the gospel and against the ministers and ordinances of Christ that any of you have been or are guilty of. For this sin provokes God to take away gospel-mercies from a people. It is true indeed—we may say and bless God for it—that for the time we have laboured among you we have met with as little of this as any have done in a place of this size. Yet some there have been that have been guilty of this, though not many; and they may have time enough to repent the hastening of their own calamities. Repent of this sin. Consider what God says of such in 2 Chronicles 36:16.

[1] That is, 'medicine,' sometimes used particularly of a laxative, as may be intended here.—P.

Repent of your unthankfulness for the gospel. Repent of your not prizing ordinances enough, of your too much loathing, or at least (even by the best) too little loving, spiritual manna.

Repent of your barrenness and unfruitfulness under, and too little improvement of, the Word, sacraments and Sabbaths you have enjoyed. Bewail your sin, that you have got no more good by all these, that you have laid up no more in your years of plenty against years of scarcity.

Repent of that too much wantonness in opinion and practice that has been found among professors under choicest gospel-enjoyments. Repent that you have played by the light and with the bread that God has vouchsafed to you, and not wrought by the one, or fed heartily upon the other, which may justly provoke God to put out your light and take away your bread.

Repent of your decays in religion and grace, for which God threatens to remove the candlestick from a church and people (*Rev.* 2:4, 5).

Lastly, repent of the deadness and formality in religion and in the worship of God, which you see to be in others, but most of all of that which you find and feel to be in your own hearts. For, for these and such like sins it is that God comes as a thief on churches or persons.

In order to stir you up to repent, consider that if you do not repent, God will come as a thief on you, even suddenly, unexpectedly, when you least think of it, and that to take away your treasure, your most precious things, which are so in themselves and should be so in your esteem, even his Word, sacraments, sabbaths, ministers, and all the tokens of his gracious presence. This will God do, if you do not repent, but remain hard-hearted and formal, still contenting yourselves with a name to live.

Consider, if you do repent of the evil you have done against God, God may, yea, you have ground to hope he will, repent of the evil he is doing unto you. He can find out ways agreeable to his Word and will to continue or restore ministers to people and people to ministers. He may yet return and leave a blessing behind him. Oh, therefore repent; let us all set upon this work of repentance.

And now, beloved, I have finished what I at this time intended to speak upon this text and probably with my testimony in public among you. Let me beseech you seriously to consider and set upon the practice of the duties I have in the name of the Lord from this scripture exhorted you to. Beloved, it is no small grief and trouble to myself and fellow-labourer to part from you. It was in our hearts to have lived and died with you and among you, if God had seen it fit; but the will of the Lord be done. We must acknowledge to the glory of God and your just commendation that great has been the encouragement we have found among you, from God, from you, and from our honourable patron. From God in his remarkable providence in bringing us first among you, in vouchsafing his gracious presence to and with us since, and in giving us some considerable fruit of our weak unworthy labours, so that we can say a great door and effectual has been opened, though of late there have been many adversaries. And great has been the encouragement we have received from you also, from your great affection to us, and especially from your ready entertainment of our labours and forward and cheerful submission to the ordinances of Christ that have been dispensed among you, which, though it cannot but add much to our grief in parting from you, yet it is no small addition to our comfort also. We have also received much encouragement and many undeserved respects from the honourable patron of this place; for all which we heartily bless God, and no less heartily pray that God would recompense his and your respects to us a thousand fold into his and your bosoms.

And I trust we can in sincerity say for ourselves that we have not sought yours but you, and that it is not the loss of our places and outward accommodations that troubles us, but the loss of our opportunities of serving our God and your precious and immortal souls in the work of the gospel. It grieves us to think of the snares and temptations you may meet with, for when the shepherds are smitten the sheep are like to be scattered. If God shall send such among you as will in the main be faithful to God and your souls, it will afford much heart-ease to us and satisfaction to our spirits. We have for above eleven years preached to you by our public labours; God now calls us and many others to preach to you by our silence. And the very silence of so many ministers, if blessed by the Lord, may prove the most powerful and effectual sermon to people that they have had. This speaks God's displeasure; this bids both us and you to look into our and your hearts and ways, to find what it is that has provoked God to send upon us this sad dispensation.

The silence of ministers calls aloud on us all to humble ourselves under the mighty hand of God. It bids us repent of our sins, the causes of God's judgments. It calls on you to prize and improve ministers and ordinances better, if God shall continue, restore or further afford them to you. Yea, ministers' silence should cause people to speak the more and louder to God in prayer for the continuance and restoring of ministers and ordinances to them. When you do not hear so much and so often from God in preaching, let God hear the more and oftener from you in prayer. Ply the throne of grace. Give God no rest till he make Jerusalem a praise in the earth. And as our silence should make you speak the more to God, so also the more and oftener one unto another in holy conference, to provoke to love and to good works. And I beseech you, brethren, pray for us. Whatever God may do with us or whithersoever we may be driven we shall carry you in our hearts; and when and while we remember ourselves to God, we shall never forget you but present you and your souls' concerns daily unto God at the throne of grace in our prayers. And we earnestly beg this of you, as you would remember what we have spoken to you in the name of the Lord, so you would remember us to God, and let us have a room and share in your hearts and prayers. When you get into a corner to pour out your hearts before God, carry us to God upon your hearts. Do not forget us, but lift up a prayer to God for us, your (we hope we may say) faithful, though weak, unworthy ministers, who have laboured among you in the Word and doctrine.

I shall say no more, but conclude with these two scriptures: 'And now, brethren, I commend you to God, and to the word of his grace, which is able to build you up, and to give you an inheritance among all them which are sanctified' (*Acts* 20:32). The other scripture is that request of Paul to, and prayer for, the Hebrews in chapter 13:18-21: 'Pray for us: for we trust we have a good conscience, in all things willing to live honestly. But I beseech you the rather to do this, that I may be restored to you the sooner. Now the God of peace, that brought again from the dead our Lord Jesus, that great shepherd of the sheep, through the blood of the everlasting covenant, make you perfect in every good work to do his will, working in you that which is well pleasing in his sight, through Jesus Christ; to whom be glory for ever and ever. Amen.'

THE NONCONFORMIST'S CATECHISM

THE NONCONFORMIST'S CATECHISM

Samuel Palmer[1]

INTRODUCTION

1. What are the grand principles on which the Protestant Nonconformists ground their separation from the Church by law established?

The right of private judgment and liberty of conscience, in opposition to all human authority in matters of religion; the supremacy of Christ as the only Head of his church, and the sufficiency of the Holy Scriptures as the only rule of faith and practice.

[1] Palmer lived 1741-1813. This catechism was first published in 1772. It has gone through many editions and been revised a number of times. The 27th edition rewritten by 'Two Cambridge Nonconformists' was published in the bicentenary year of the Ejection. From the 29th edition which appeared in 1890 to the present time we can find no record of a reprint other than the Trust's 1962 edition in this form, which was abridged and revised from the 16th issue, printed in 1818. Various footnotes have been added by the present publishers.

2. Does the Scripture not require us to be subject to the civil magistrate, as 'the minister of God' for conscience' sake?

Yes, doubtless, in all civil affairs, but not in matters of religion, much less in things contrary to the law of God, so that all human laws which are inconsistent with the divine ought to be disobeyed.

3. But is every man to judge for himself whether the laws of his country are agreeable to the laws of God?

Certainly, in the affairs of religion, every man ought to judge for himself, since every man must render an account of himself to God, who has given us an infallible rule in his Word to guide us and the promise of the teaching of his Spirit to enable the believer to understand for himself the way of truth and duty.

4. But are we not required in Scripture to obey our spiritual rulers who have a juster claim to implicit faith and unlimited obedience than civil magistrates?

The Word of God expressly forbids Christians giving up conscience to the directions of any man;[1] and the apostles themselves disclaimed all dominion over it,[2] and urged it upon their hearers to examine and judge for themselves.[3]

[1] 'Call no man your Father upon the earth . . . neither be ye called masters, for one is your Master, even Christ' (*Matt.* 23:9, 10). 'In vain they do worship me, teaching for doctrines the commandments of men' (*Matt.* 15:9).

[2] 'Not for that we have dominion over your faith, but are helpers of your joy' (2 *Cor.* 1:24). 'Neither as being lords over God's heritage, but being ensamples to the flock' (*1 Pet.* 5:3).

[3] 'These [Berean Jews] were more noble than those in

5. ***Ought we not to be very cautious how we separate from a Christian and Protestant Church?***

Doubtless it is not every trifling circumstance that will justify separations among Christians. But the Nonconformists apprehend that the grounds of their separation from the Church of England are so many and so important as to fully warrant such action.

6. ***What are the principal things in the Church of England on which the dissent from it is founded?***

1) Its general frame and constitution as national and established by law.

2) The character and authority of certain officers appointed in it.

3) The imposition of a stated form of prayer, called the liturgy, and many exceptionable things contained therein.

4) The pretended right of enjoining unscriptural ceremonies.

5) The want of liberty in the people to choose their own ministers.

6) The corrupt state of its discipline.

Thessalonica, in that they . . . searched the scriptures daily, whether those things were so' (*Acts* 17:11). 'I speak as to wise men; judge ye what I say' (*1 Cor.* 10:15). 'Let every man be fully persuaded in his own mind' (*Rom.* 14:5). 'Prove all things; hold fast that which is good' (*1 Thess.* 5:21).

1: THE GENERAL FRAME AND CONSTITUTION OF THE CHURCH OF ENGLAND

7. What do the Nonconformists believe to be the scriptural idea of a church of Christ?

A congregation, or voluntary society of Christians, who commonly meet together to attend gospel ordinances in the same place. And they think every such society has a right to transact its own affairs according to the judgment and conscience of the members thereof, without being accountable to any but Jesus Christ or restrained by any laws but his.

8. How does it appear that this notion of a church of Christ is the scriptural one?

A number of Christians assembled for divine worship in a dwelling-house is in Scripture called a church.[1] A church is spoken of as coming together in one place.[2] When affairs were to be determined relating to a church, all the members were called together to give their opinion.[3] And we do not find any superior authority acknowledged or claimed.

9. What do the Nonconformists object to in the general constitution of the Church of England?

Because it is a civil establishment, framed by human

[1] 'Greet the church that is in their house' (*Rom.* 16:5; see also *1 Cor.* 16:19, *Philem.* 2). It is observable that the several congregations of Christians in the same province are spoken of, not in the singular, but the plural number: e.g., the churches of Judæa, the churches of Galatia, *etc.*

[2] 1 Corinthians 14:23.

[3] Acts 6:2, 5; 15:4, 22.

authority—its laws founded on Acts of Parliament and the chief magistrate, as such, being its supreme head. Whereas a church of Christ according to the scriptural account of it, is a society of persons united solely on religious views,[1] whose laws are no other than the Word of God,[2] which they have a right to interpret for themselves, and whose supreme and only Head is Jesus Christ.[3]

10. What power has the king in the Church of England, which constitutes him its supreme head?

The king (or queen) 'is vested with all power to exercise all manner of ecclesiastical jurisdiction; and archbishops, bishops, archdeacons, and other ecclesiastical persons, have no manner of jurisdiction ecclesiastical, but by and under the king's majesty, who hath full power and authority to hear and determine all manner of causes ecclesiastical, and to reform and correct all vice, sin, errors, and heresies whatsoever.'[4]

The appointing of bishops also is his prerogative.

11. What objection have Nonconformists to this authority of the sovereign?

Though they think it their duty to honour and obey the sovereign in civil matters, they apprehend such power as our present constitution gives him in affairs of religion to be not only foreign to the province of the

[1] John 17:16; 18:36.
[2] Psalm 19:7, Ephesians 2:20.
[3] Ephesians 1:22 .
[4] These are the words of the 1534 Act of Supremacy (Act 26 Henry VIII Cap. 1). See also the royal declaration prefixed to the *39 Articles* and, in particular, Article 37.

civil magistrate, but highly derogatory to the honour of Christ, whom God has appointed 'head over all things to the church,' and a gross infringement on the liberty of Christians, who, in matters of faith and conscience, are forbidden to be the servants of men.[1]

12. May it not be of service to religion to have the authority of the chief magistrate on its side?

The religion of Jesus does not need the support of human power; his church is founded on a rock more stable than any earthly establishment and the gates of hell shall never prevail against it.[2] The interference of the civil magistrate in affairs of religion has often been more injurious than beneficial, and this authority in matters of faith is exceedingly dangerous.

13. Did religion ever flourish in a nation where it was not established?

The religion of Jesus, as established in the hearts of men, never flourished more than when it had (as at first) all the powers of the earth engaged against it.

[1] 'Ye are bought with a price; be not ye the servants of men' (*1 Cor*. 7:23).

[2] Matthew 16:18.

2: THE OFFICERS APPOINTED IN THE CHURCH OF ENGLAND

14. What officers are employed in the Church of England to whom Nonconformists object?

Archbishops, diocesan bishops, archdeacons, deans, prebendaries, canons, minor canons, chancellors, vicars-general, commissaries, surrogates, proctors, *etc.*, offices which Christ never appointed, and which nothing in the New Testament warrants, but are the effect of an unnatural alliance of the church with the state, and mostly of popish origin.

15. How many orders of ministers are there in the Church of England?

Three: bishops, priests, and deacons, for which the Nonconformists apprehend there is no scriptural warrant. The bishops we read of in the New Testament were no other than the pastors of particular congregations, often called elders or presbyters. The term priest is never therein applied to ministers as distinct from other Christians, the priestly office (since Christ once offered up himself) being for ever abolished. The scriptural deacons are not ministers of the gospel but officers appointed to take care of the temporal needs of poor.[1]

16. What have you to object to in the superiority of the bishops over the clergy?

No such distinction of ministers is appointed by Christ in his church, but on the contrary, he has expressly forbidden

[1] See Acts 6.

any of them to assume dominion over the rest.[1] And as to the office of an archbishop, none pretend to produce any scriptural warrant for it.

17. Is there not something exceptionable in the manner of making a bishop?

There is a great deal of pomp and parade in this business, which is carried out through the following procedure: (1) The prime minister nominates certain names to the crown. (2) The queen forwards to the dean and chapter of the cathedral of the diocese concerned the *congé d'élire*—her licence giving permission to elect—with the name of the man chosen by the crown and instructions to the chapter to elect him. (3) The crown instructs the archbishop of the province to confirm the election. (4) The archbishop consecrates the new bishop. (5) The bishop is enthroned in the cathedral church of his diocese, marking 'the ceremonial and public entry of the new bishop into his cathedral and diocese.' (6) The bishop must pay homage to the queen before he can possess the income and property of his see.

18. What is objected to in the manner of ordination by bishops?

They require all whom they ordain to declare that they are moved by the Holy Ghost in undertaking the

[1] See Matthew 20:25-27, 'Ye know that the princes of the Gentiles exercise dominion over them . . . but it shall not be so among you: but whosoever will be great among you, let him be your minister.' Also Matthew 23:8–9, 'Be not ye called Rabbi: for one is your Master, even Christ; and all ye are brethren. And call no man your father upon earth: for one is your Father, which is in heaven.'

ministerial office, and then pretend, or seem as if they pretended, to confer the Holy Spirit by the imposition of their hands, saying, 'Receive the Holy Ghost for the Office and Work of a Priest in the Church of God.'

19. Can any officiate as ministers in the Church of England who have not been ordained by her own bishops?

No; all other ordination is viewed as invalid, excepting that of the Roman Catholics, who, if they conform to the Church of England, are not required to be re-ordained.

20. What is the common argument for the exclusive right of the bishops to ordain?

That they have derived it by uninterrupted succession from the apostles.

21. What is the objection to this right by uninterrupted succession?

The Scriptures nowhere mention it as necessary to render ordination valid. The Church of England cannot prove that she is possessed of it and, if she could, she must have received it through the corrupt channel of the Church of Rome.

22. What is the nature and design of the rite of confirmation, as performed by the bishops?

It is designed for young persons thereby to take upon themselves the vow which their sponsors made in their name at their baptism.

23. *What does the bishop perform on these occasions?*

He thanks God for having regenerated them by water and the Holy Ghost and forgiven all their sins. He then lays his hand upon the head of every person and 'certifies them all, by that sign, of God's favour, and gracious goodness towards them.'

24. *What is required of persons in order to their being thus confirmed?*

Nothing more than their having a certificate from their minister that they can say the Lord's Prayer, the Creed, the Ten Commandments, and the Catechism, and their answering *all together* in the affirmative, to the question, 'Do ye . . . renew the solemn promise and vow that was made in your name at your Baptism?'

25. *What do Nonconformists object to in this ceremony?*

They believe that it has no foundation in Scripture, and is attended with very dangerous consequences. Besides, should the propriety of the rite itself be allowed, every parish minister seems to be as capable of performing it as a bishop.

26. *What dangerous consequence is likely to arise from this rite?*

Ignorant people, who have too good an opinion of the bishop to think he would declare a falsehood, are likely to look upon themselves to be what he has declared they are—pardoned, regenerated, and interested in God's favour—and so conclude their state is safe, while yet they continue in their sins.

3: THE LITURGY

27. What is the mode of worship in the established Church?

A stated form of prayer is used, called the liturgy, or Common Prayer.

28. Do Nonconformists think forms of prayer in themselves sinful?

No; they think it far better to pray by a form than not at all or in an indecent, incoherent manner, but do not approve of the use of a liturgy or stated form in public worship.

29. What are the leading objections made against liturgies in general?

1) That the Scripture is silent with respect to the necessity or expediency of them, and we have no example whatever in the New Testament of Christians using a set form of prayer.

2) It seems inconsistent with the work of the Holy Spirit that Christian ministers who are endowed by him for the exercise of their work should be confined to an invariable form in their prayers.

30. What is objected to the liturgy of the Church of England in particular?

1) That it is imposed by human authority, so that ministers must make no variation from it, whatever the peculiar circumstances of things may require; and no alteration can be made in it, however proper and necessary, without an Act of Parliament.

2) That there are many things objectionable in the liturgy itself, e.g., in the general form and construction of it, in the sentiment in several particular parts, and frequently in the language.

31. What is objectionable as to sentiment in particular parts of the liturgy?

1) *In the office of baptism.* Such expressions are used concerning the efficacy of that rite, as naturally lead persons to conceive of it as a saving ordinance, which, however, is rendered ridiculous by the questions put to the infant in the person of the sponsors and the answers they make in its name, concerning its faith and future conduct.

2) *In the visitation of the sick.* After the sick person has declared his assent to the Articles of the Creed and professed his repentance and his charity with all men, he is to be 'moved to make a special confession of his sins, if he feels his conscience troubled.' After which confession, the Priest is required, 'if he humbly and heartily desire it,' to absolve him.

3) *In the Burial Service.* One service is read at all funerals, without distinction; whatever the age, circumstances,

or character of the deceased may be even though some are known to have died unbelievers and without any signs of repentance; those only are excluded from the burial service who were unbaptized, self-murderers, or excommunicated. In this service, the minister is required to style the deceased, 'Our dear brother,' to express a sure and certain hope of his resurrection to eternal life, and to thank God for having taken him out of the miseries of this sinful world. Such expressions, because of the relaxation of church discipline, must often hurt the consciences of ministers. It is also attended with very dangerous consequences with respect to the people, who may naturally encourage themselves to go on in sin on the presumption of obtaining happiness at last, as they so often hear worldly persons when dead pronounced eternally happy.

4) *In the Use of Apocryphal Books.* From whence lessons are appointed to be publicly read, and that in place of some part of the inspired writings, which seems to give the Apocrypha equal authority with the Bible. Some of these lessons contain the most ridiculous stories in the whole book.

32. How is it to be accounted for that there are so many exceptionable things in the liturgy?

The plain reason is the greater part of it was taken from the old popish liturgy, from which the first Reformers prudently made as little variation as possible. But their successors, resting satisfied with what they had done, have made no material alteration since.

4: CEREMONIES

33. What is the opinion of Nonconformists respecting ceremonies in divine worship?

They disapprove of such as are of human invention, especially when their use is made obligatory in worship, and they think themselves bound to refuse complying with them.

34. Are there ceremonies in the Church of England that are forbidden in Scripture?

That a ceremony is not expressly forbidden by Scripture does not warrant its practice, because the scriptural rule excludes all religious ceremonies that are not of divine appointment.[1] Their not being commanded is therefore a sufficient reason for refusing them.

35. Does not the Church of England claim authority to decree rites and ceremonies in divine worship?

Yes, expressly, in the 20th of the *39 Articles*, which commences, 'The Church hath power to decree Rites or Ceremonies,' but Nonconformists deny the claim and cannot submit to any of her ceremonies till she can prove her authority to enjoin them from Scripture.

36. Is nothing to be required in the worship of God but what is commanded in Scripture?

Nothing but what is either expressly commanded or necessarily implied in a command.

[1] See Colossians 2:20-23, 'Why . . . are ye subject to ordinances . . . after the commandments and doctrines of men? Which things have indeed a shew of wisdom in will worship, and humility.'

37. Are not these ceremonies indifferent? What then can be the harm of complying with them?

Though they be allowed indifferent in themselves, they may not be so in all the circumstances of them; and if they were indifferent they cease to be so when their observation is made obligatory and they become terms of Christian communion.

38. What harm can there be in submitting to authority in things indifferent for the sake of peace?

It would be acknowledging in those who have assumed the office of government in the Church, a right that Christ never gave them, the pretension to which is derogatory to his honour; and it would be giving up that 'liberty wherewith Christ has made us free' and in which we are exhorted to stand fast.[1]

39. Are any harmful consequences likely to arise from those few ceremonies that the Church of England has appointed?

They can do no good and may be abused to bad purposes. They tend to destroy the simplicity of divine worship; they encourage superstition and lead the way to popery, which abounds with human inventions.

40. But does not the Church of England disclaim the errors of popery?

It does so in words, but not in fact, so long as it claims authority in matters of faith, or a right to decree ceremonies.

[1] Galatians 5:1.

Those ceremonies that it uses are of popish origin, and upon the same principle that it adopts these, it might admit all the rest.

41. What are the ceremonies used in the Church of England to which there is objection?

(1) Bowing towards the east. (2) Bowing at the name of Jesus. (3) Signing with a cross in baptism. (4) Particular gestures in worship, especially kneeling at the Lord's supper.

42. What is the ceremony of bowing to the east?

The communion-table is generally placed at the east end of the church and to it rigid Churchmen turn their faces when they say the Creed and bow when they come to the name of Jesus Christ.

43. What is the special objection to this ceremony?

That the communion-table has no more sanctity in it than any other table, and that the custom of bowing towards it had its rise in popery, which teaches that the bread and wine placed upon it are the very body and blood of Christ, which thing the Church of England professes, with all other Protestants, to deny.

44. What is the pretence for the priest's crossing the forehead in baptism?

It is said to be done as a token that the person baptized 'shall not be ashamed to confess the faith of Christ crucified, and manfully to fight under his banner.'

45. What is objected to in this ceremony?

1) That Christ never appointed it.

2) If an outward mark of the cross must be used as a badge of a disciple of Christ, it ought either to be visible and permanent or often repeated, as it is by the Papists.

3) To use any ceremony in baptism as a token of the cross or sufferings of Christ is to make this ordinance interfere with the design of the Lord's supper, in which bread and wine are divinely appointed to be memorials of his sufferings and the receiving of them is the outward expression of the believer's readiness to confess Christ crucified.

4) Making this ceremony essential to the administration of baptism is an unreasonable and unjust imposition on the consciences of those who might scruple at it.

46. What is there objectionable in the Church respecting gestures in divine worship?

The Church authoritatively requires the people to be continually changing their postures—to stand in particular parts of the service, to kneel in others, and to sit in others—when neither Scripture nor reason point out the difference. They are always required to kneel at receiving the sacrament.

47. Is the posture of Nonconformists at the Lord's supper the same that our Lord and his disciples used?

No, but it is certain that they used the same posture in which they received their common meals. The Nonconformists therefore believe that as sitting is the common table posture now, they come the nearest to our Saviour's pattern in using it at his table. This is most suitable to the idea of the Lord's supper as a feast; and it was doubtless the converting of the table into an altar that introduced the custom of kneeling at it.

48. Are there not some other ceremonies observed in the Church of England?

There are several customs that partake of the nature of ceremonies, and are liable to much the same objections—e.g., wearing particular habits, observing certain days as holy, the distinction of places, and the use of sponsors in baptism—all which are mere human and arbitrary appointments.

49. What is the opinion of the Nonconformists on the wearing of particular habits?

They consider them as relics of popish superstition, particularly the surplice. But they especially object to the imposition of any kind of dress in the worship of God, though they do not conceive one form or colour of a garment to be in itself sinful more than another.

50. What days does the Church appoint to be kept holy?

No less than 150 in the year, besides the Lord's day, *viz.*, 29 Feasts, 16 Vigils, (or fasts before holy-days), 40 fasts in Lent, 12 Ember-days, 3 Rogation-days, 4 Solemn days, and all Fridays in the year (excepting Christmas Day).

51. What do Nonconformists object to the appointment of these holy days?

1) Such observances encourage superstition and will-worship and are a tacit reflection on the great head of the Church, who has required no day to be kept holy but the weekly sabbath.

2) Some passages in Scripture strongly discourage them; especially Galatians 4:9-11. 'How turn ye again to the weak and beggarly elements . . . ? Ye observe days, and months, and times, and years. I am afraid of you, lest I have bestowed upon you labour in vain.'

52. What is particularly objected to in the observation of Saints-days?

It looks like the adoration of departed spirits as practised in the Church of Rome and thus leads to popery, as it evidently sprang from thence.

53. What are the chief objections against the office of sponsors?

1) It excludes the parents who bear the primary responsibility for the spiritual instruction and upbringing of their own children.

2) It is making a human addition to an ordinance of Christ and a new condition of receiving it, for none can be baptized in the Church of England without sponsors.

5: THE CHOICE OF MINISTERS

54. How are congregations supplied with ministers in the Church of England?

Many livings, as they are called, are in the gift of the king (as all the bishoprics in effect are), some of the Lord Chancellor, some of the bishops, and some of the universities, but with many others belonging to different individuals or parties. Every person having a living in his gift (who is called the patron) may present whom he pleases to it, and the people have no spiritual liberty to prevent the settlement of a minister, nor the bishop to refuse giving institution and induction, except in a few cases.

55. How do Nonconformists think that congregations should be supplied with ministers?

They think that no person whatsoever is authorised to impose a minister upon others, but that every congregation has a right to choose its own[1] and to judge the lawfulness of his calling by comparison with the scriptural marks of a faithful minister of Christ.[2]

[1] When an apostle was to be chosen in the room of Judas the whole body of the disciples was applied to on the occasion (*Acts* 1). And even the seven deacons were not chosen by the apostles but by the whole multitude (*Acts* 6).

[2] Ministers are spoken of as the servants of the church (2 *Cor.* 4:5). Christians are exhorted not to believe every spirit but to try the spirits whether they are of God (*1 John* 4:1), to beware of false prophets (*Matt.* 24:24), and to take heed what they hear (*Luke* 8:18).

6: CHURCH DISCIPLINE

56. What is objected to in the discipline of the established Church?

That it is shamefully defective and corrupt, particularly in the admission of persons to the Lord's table and in the administration of baptism to the children of parents who are not Christians.

57. Whom does the Church admit to the Lord's table?

No persons whatever are refused who have been confirmed by the bishop and are not excommunicated.

58. May not the minister refuse those who are known to be worldly characters?

No. Though the rubric orders the clergy to 'advertise any evil-liver, that he presume not to come to the Lord's table,' the most infamous sinner in the parish, if he should be refused, may appeal to the Ecclesiastical Court; and if he can secure the favour of the chancellor, he may secure admission, and defy the minister to exclude him.

59. What would be the consequence if a minister should conscientiously persist in refusing the sacrament to an unworthy person?

He would be liable to suspension for such refusal and, if he would not comply, to excommunication.

60. But does the Church suffer no notice to be taken of the immorality of its members?

Yes; but neither the minister of the parish, nor any of the congregation, can exercise any sort of discipline; their offences must be brought before the spiritual court, where chancellors are the judges, who are often laymen, whose determination will stand in law, though contrary to that of the bishop.

7: INFERENCES FROM THE WHOLE

61. What inferences may be drawn from the foregoing account of the Church of England?

1) That the Church of England is imperfectly reformed from popery and still bears too strong resemblance to the Church of Rome.

2) That therefore it behoves those who have power in the Church to exert themselves in order to carry on the reformation and endeavour to perfect what the first reformers so nobly begun, with greater difficulty and hazard than their successors have in the present day any reason to fear, so that the Church of England may truly and consistently call herself Protestant.

3) That while those on whom this work properly devolves will take no steps towards a further reform but, on the contrary, are determined to keep things as they are, it is the indispensable duty of those who are dissatisfied with them and whose consciences would be uneasy with conformity in a peaceable manner to dissent.

4) That the Nonconformists ought to be exceedingly thankful to God for the liberty they enjoy of separating from a national Church, which they think so corrupt, and of worshipping God in places of their own in a manner agreeable to the dictates of their consciences and, as they think, to the rules of God's holy Word, at the same time sympathising with and praying for those of their Protestant brethren abroad who are deprived of this privilege.

5) That they ought to be steadfast in their adherence to the cause of Nonconformity, zealous in maintaining the great principles of it, and active to support and increase it by all such methods as are consistent with peace, liberty, and charity, still making it to appear that their zeal is principally directed to the cause of practical godliness and the interest of Christ at large, even in that Church from which they dissent.

They should love good men of every name and rejoice wheresoever 'Christ is preached and God is worshipped in spirit,' though the mode be different from their own, making all proper allowance for the prejudices of education, which often have too great influence on the best of men. But a true catholic spirit does not require men to give up their own principles or be indifferent to the support of them, nor ought we to conform to unscriptural modes or submit to human impositions merely because they are approved by many whom we believe to be eminent for piety or to hold the fundamental doctrines of the gospel.

SERMONS OF THE GREAT EJECTION

If the principles of dissent from the national Church be of any importance (and whether they be or not, let the foregoing pages determine) surely those Nonconformists act a very inconsistent part, who are indifferent to them, many of whom seem to forget that their forefathers, whom they profess to venerate, left the national Church on account of those impositions on conscience which strike at the headship of Jesus Christ and which this Church still continues to practise. And doubtless it is incumbent on those who are convinced of the truth of those principles on which their own nonconformity is founded to take care that their children be well instructed in the knowledge of them.

THE BANNER OF TRUTH TRUST

3 Murrayfield Road
Edinburgh, EH12 6EL
UK

PO Box 621, Carlisle
Pennsylvania, 17013
USA

www.banneroftruth.co.uk